BALM *for* GILEAD

BALM *for* GILEAD

Pastoral Care for African American Families Experiencing Abuse

Toinette M. Eugene and James N. Poling

Abingdon Press
Nashville

Library of Congress Cataloging-in-Publication Data

Eugene, Toinette M., 1945-
    Balm for Gilead : pastoral care for African American families experiencing abuse / Toinette M. Eugene and James N. Poling.
    p. cm.
    Includes bibliographical references and index.
    ISBN 0-687-02347-5 (pbk. : alk. paper)
    1. Church work with Afro-American families. 2. Church work with problem families. 3. Afro-American families—Pastoral counseling of. 4. Problem families—Pastoral counseling of. 5. Family violence—Religious aspects—Christianity. I. Poling, James N. (James Newton), 1942– II. Title.
BV4468.A34E94   1998
259'.1'08996073—dc21

98-20646
CIP

*Dedicated with profound gratitude
to those brave black women and men
whose stories of survival recorded in this book
have been offered as a "Balm for Gilead"
to all those who will come after.*

CONTENTS

ACKNOWLEDGMENTS

Special thanks to the African American victims and survivors who, over many years, have entrusted their stories and encouraged us to write about the religious resources available for healing.

Special Thanks to Marie Fortune, Emilie Townes, and the many other womanist and feminist scholars who have contributed wonderfully constructive critical and pastoral reflection to our work over the years. [TME and JNP]

Special thanks to J. Deotis Roberts, Isabel Boutte Kellum, and Jennifer S. Simpson, who have sustained and supported my study of African American families and the black church as a liberation ministry. [TME]

Special thanks to Gilbert Bond, Donald Matthews, Thelma Burgonio-Watson, Nancy Werking Poling and others who gave me critical feedback at crucial points in my growing understanding of abuse and healing. [JNP]

INTRODUCTION

This book is about the faith-filled lives of black families
who have experienced abuse and about the caring responses from the church communities who are responsible
for providing the healing balm for Gilead that these victims
and their violators so sorely need. It portrays the courage,
creativity, and resilience of members of black families who
have dared to break the silence that surrounds sexual abuse
and domestic violence in order to disclose the God who
wills resistance to evil in all its forms. For purposes of vin-
dication and transformation we present the worldviews of
African American women and men who have begun to tell
their stories of abuse at the hands of family members, relatives, neighbors, and others who used their relational roles
to prey on those who were vulnerable or over whom they
could exert abusive power.

Sexual abuse, physical child abuse, family violence, and
homicides are arguably among the most serious social problems in the black community and thus justify the current
level of public and professional concern. Because of increasing family violence which stems from racial, class, and gen-
der-based misunderstanding and conflict, it is time to respond more definitively to the crisis that African American
victims and survivors are facing. Although the problem of
family violence has existed for generations, only recently has
it begun to receive from the Christian church and from pastoral care givers, social service agencies, and social justice
advocates the attention that it deserves. Encouraged and
empowered by the model of the historic black church, which

traditionally has always offered its members a "balm for Gilead," we have undertaken this work of responding to the needs of both those who suffer from the worst wounds the world can inflict, and to the needs of those who are called and chosen to be healers, leaders, pastors, and teachers of those persons who embody the vision and the future of the black family as a "domestic church."

This book is about churches and religious institutions in or accessible to the black community that have begun to hear and take seriously the stories of victims and survivors of family violence, to respond to these calls for justice, and to hold abusers accountable. Here we affirm pastoral, professional, and prophetic leaders who serve and sustain the victims and survivors of black family violence, and we encourage those who minister to their violators to do their work in renewed ways—ways that are able to transform that which has been meant as evil into good in the form of renewed black family relationships.

The thesis of this book is that an informed and authentic ethic of care, provided by pastoral, prophetic, and therapeutic leaders in the black faith community, is the principal means for transforming the pain of family violence into redemptive black love. Such love is expressed in and through the life of the institutional church and its members. We are well aware that the black faith community, united in its support for victims, its abhorrence of abuse, and its commitment to justice, has been divided in its understandings of which definitions of abuse are appropriate. We know that research on black family violence has raised questions about the nature of the ethical practice of those in the helping professions and those who are actively engaged in healing relationships in the communities within which they live, work, and worship.

As practical theologians and as persons committed to equipping religious institutions to minister effectively to

both victims and offenders of sexual and domestic violence,[1] we have no easy answers that resolve all these concerns. Instead, in these pages you will find an extended
conversation between social ethics and the field of pastoral
care. You will find a dialogue born of our frustration and
anger at the ways in which the lives of countless black family members have not found relief and have not found a
balm that soothes as well as cures because those who are
responsible for their care have not received sufficient training and preparation to allow them to minister in ways that
transform and liberate from the sorrow of untenable situations.

We hope this text provides some of the missing elements
of culturally sensitive theological education for seminari-
ans and continuing education for pastoral leaders and
caregivers in the black community. Here you will find a dialogue between a black womanist ethicist and a white male
pastoral theologian that has only begun. This collaboration
takes its lead and direction from those whose suffering has
inspired us. We continue to articulate our hope that the
balm for Gilead will be made more accessible for all those
who know the pain of family violence.

In this text we rely upon and use the content and
methodology of a womanist-based social, theological, and
ethical analysis as trustworthy guides for interpreting the
experience of abuse in black families and offering a praxis
that is both biblically based and liberation oriented. We
subscribe to a womanist[2] approach because it alone, of all
the analyses available to us, provides a sufficient tridimen-
sional critique of the oppressions of race, sex, and class and
adequately demolishes negatively defining social
constructions and images used against black women and
their family units. In our ongoing chapter discussions, as
well as in our conclusions, we strongly recommend the
context and methodology of a womanist-based analysis be-

cause it establishes a sound theological and Christological basis and balm for transforming the multiple abuses of power regularly visited upon vulnerable individuals into situations and circumstances that are equally redemptive and restorative of black family life.

Balm for Gilead: Pastoral Care for African American Families Experiencing Abuse has evolved structurally and stylistically out of a process of dialogue and collaboration in which we have tried to acknowledge and honor our cultural, gender, and denominational differences and to make good use of our common background, understandings, and experiences as seminary professors, social activists, and pastoral ministers. Our intent is not to synthesize obvious conclusions or to argue for true, correct positions beyond existing contradictions and differences. Thus, in what we write as black and as white, as a woman and as a man, as a Roman Catholic and as a Protestant, as a professional layperson directing an executive program in a West Coast diocesan chancery office and as an ordained clergyperson working in a Midwestern Protestant seminary, we are not homogenized in every way. Rather, we have blended and harmonized our knowledge and differences to preserve the richness of our gifts in pursuit of the common good.

We obviously write from our very different histories, families of origin, and cultural heritages. But we also speak to each other from those histories, cultures, and other worlds of difference. The book itself has been a process of learning how to hear each other's histories and learning what we need to spell out to make our own personal, professional, social, and theological positions understood. In order for the reader to understand something of the complexity of the dialogue and have a sense of the interplay between us, it is important to introduce ourselves a bit more to give a context for this work.

Introduction of Ourselves

Because we believe that pastoral theology, pastoral care, and the expression of sound social ethics requires interdisciplinary research, we initially embarked on this project through jointly teaching a class on racism and sexism at Colgate Rochester Divinity School in Rochester, New York, where we were colleagues in a community of scholars who took seriously the contributions of Black Church Studies to the entire enterprise of theological education. In the crucible of our classroom, where the praxis wheel[3] of experience, analysis, reflection, and preparation for action was regularly spun, we were forced to reflect together from the experiences of our students. We discovered that the predominant experiences from which they entered the arena of our course on racism and sexism were far too often the violence generated in their family life.

This phenomenon of a violent family life seemed to occur with unfailing regularity. The complexities and particularities added by the layers of pain reported by black students in class made us wonder what it was about the violence they knew that could be examined and perhaps eradicated by an attentive ethic of care and pastoral care praxis. The combination of our ongoing research and writing on family violence, and the realities of our students' lives suggested a book on the subject might make a difference in people's lives. Moreover, our accountability to the community of victims and survivors of domestic violence and sexual abuse with whom we work and to whom we have ministered compelled our further efforts to review what we were learning again and in more depth. And so we set to work. Our hope and prayer for this volume is that the lives and ministry of those victims, survivors, students, pastors, and professional caregivers who instructed, informed, and challenged us will benefit from our exploration of their struggles, sacrifice, and engagement in the liberation of black families from the pain of sexual violence and domestic abuse.

Toinette Eugene is a womanist of faith, rooted and grounded in the black church tradition and the Roman Catholic perspective, an ethicist, and a cross-cultural consultant. She is the Formation Director for the Pastoral Leadership Placement Board and the Director of the African American Pastoral Center of the Roman Catholic Diocese of Oakland, California. Often engaged as a facilitator for educational and ministerial conferences, she frequently gives lectures, retreats, and seminars sponsored by international, ecumenical, and interfaith institutes. Most recently she has served as associate professor of Christian social ethics at Garrett-Evangelical Theological Seminary and as a member of the graduate faculty of Northwestern University in Evanston, Illinois.

With her community of feminist and womanist colleagues, Toinette has shared the challenges that come from addressing the infrastructures of racism and sexism. She has contributed to the ethical and social analysis that is necessary to confront institutional and personal injustice which stems from resistance to change. In her own inimitable way, she has been a model and mentor for newer scholars and pastors seeking to learn the dangerous art of going into the gaps to understand the concrete demands of social justice, to practice radical theory, and to occasionally engage in what may seem at first glance to be a kind of risky or unorthodox practice.

James Poling is a pastor, professor, writer, and a leader in conferences for the church and the academy. He is currently professor of pastoral care, counseling, and theology at Garrett-Evangelical Theological Seminary and a member of the graduate faculty of Northwestern University in Evanston, Illinois. He is a member of the Presbytery of Chicago, Presbyterian Church (USA), and a pastoral counselor. He often does workshops and lectures for local churches, seminaries, and international academic conferences.

For twelve years, James has worked as a pastoral counselor with families from a variety of cultural and class backgrounds who have experienced family violence, including African American families. He has consulted with African American congregations as they have responded to the needs of victims and survivors of family violence, and has submitted his own work to African American scholars for mutual accountability. He has struggled in his own life with the influences of sexism and racism, and has confronted leaders and institutions in the white community, challenging them to purge themselves of these evils. He believes that intercultural and cross-gender cooperation is one of the most important paths to justice and to personal and institutional transformation in the white churches.

Summary of Chapters

Answers come because questions are raised. This book, and the research behind it, raises questions and highlights correlations between the external environments and internal operations for black families victimized by violence. Although there are some similarities between the black and nonblack communities regarding sexual abuse and domestic violence, the significant differences are made more complex and critical because of the history of slavery, racial violence, and racial discrimination. We know that these patterned differences in rate, nature, severity, and consequences of black family abuse and violence are created in part because of the historical and contemporary factors in the social ecology of black family life. Individual and institutional racism are important contextual variables for the study of all aspects of the black family in the United States.

The distinctive visibility, if not vulnerability, of poor, socially marginal black families cannot be separated from the substantial bias that at times results in the application of onerous labels and unequal treatment. One cannot argue, however, that family violence among blacks is caused exclusively by racism; some important variables mediate the effects of racism and other external factors on families. The chapters show that responsibility for violence in black families resides as much in the society and in the churches as in the relationships among family members. Such issues addressed here seem to us to be of pressing concern to pastoral leaders and other professionals who study black family life and who work to alleviate black family violence, as well as to those advocates in the civic, religious, and educational communities who provide social services and social justice to black families.

Chapter 1 therefore explores sociotheological perspectives of the black family and a historical review of the black family as a domestic expression of the black church. In order to establish a framework for pastoral care, the black church must offer a balm that is therapeutic, theological, and theoretical enough to provide an effective practical remedy for domestic violence and sexual abuse. In chapter 2, we examine the impact of racism, sexism, and classism on the ongoing formation of the black family. This social analysis is crucial in order to offset the pathological scholarship that has blamed the victims for their circumstances and condemned the survivors to situations of self-hatred and social stigmas that reinforce the injustice of their shame, segregation, and second-class citizenship in both religious and secular settings.

Chapter 3 discusses the nature of sexual violence and domestic abuse in dialogue with the literature on the black family in order to better comprehend the sources of support resident or nascent within the black church and the black communities to which victims and survivors most readily turn for help in times of trouble. We attempt to bring the wisdom from the general debate about family violence into dialogue with discussion by black scholars about the nature of African American families in order to better understand the causes and consequences of abuse within this context.

The stories of six persons who have experienced severe abuse are recounted in chapter 4 to give detail and description to the chapters that precede and follow this centerpiece. The vignettes of these courageous individuals, women and men, are offered as mirrors of family abuse, mired in the effects of racism and sexism, and revelatory of the ambiguous role of the black church in responding to the pain and suffering which these members of black families endured. We believe that when pastoral strategies and ethical values are proposed and presented by seminary professors, professional caregivers, and other persons concerned about the effects of violence and abuse, it is critical that the voices and experiences of those most directly and deeply affected not become displaced by "experts" on the issues. We follow the principle that the experiences of those oppressed in a particular situation have hermeneutical privilege to be heard and to help shape the nature of the debate.[4]

Chapter 5 presents a pastoral analysis of the abuse experienced by the victims in the preceding chapter. We show that sexual abuse and domestic violence lead to confusion about faith and belief in the lives of its victims. We believe that identifying the forms of resistance to the violence can help pastoral leaders to become more astute about the nature and existence of family violence itself and more skilled and proactive in establishing methods of prevention through the ministries of the church.

In chapter 6 we discuss how pastoral care givers to the black church and black family can offer effective interventions with victims and survivors of violence abuse. The privileged position of pastors and religious leaders within the black faith community becomes a means by which the roles of those individuals can be used in order to offer the balm of anointing and affirming care, which may restore the living dead to a life worth living and sharing with others. Principles of pastoral care for victims and survivors are elaborated in detail and in relation to legal and social service systems which are also required and expected to protect those at risk.

Because the black church historically has been a family for those who have needed a "father to the fatherless and a mother to the motherless," the traditional theology of the believing community has never turned away errant members or wayward believers from a place that might provide a forum for restitution, reconciliation, and a chance to change from a past that has been destructive. For this reason, and because of the reality that where there are victims there are perpetrators, chapter 7 is a forum to discuss pastoral interventions with perpetrators of abuse. Working with perpetrators requires significant revision in the definition and practice of pastoral care and pastoral theology in order to provide safety for victims and accountability for perpetrators.

Chapter 8 offers models, suggestions, and examples of corporate pastoral care; congregational responses; and educational and prevention strategies for use by churches who minister to African American families experiencing abuse. Concurring with the insights of others writing on and offering models for pastoral care and pastoral ministry in the black church,[5] we know that established premier models insist that the expertise and energy of the entire congregation is necessary to sustain effective pastoral response. Chapter 9 offers our concluding ethical reflections and insights for those who are themselves the source of the balm for Gilead. An ethic of care is described in order to give shape and focus to the ongoing ministry of justice and healing for black families.

CHAPTER ONE

The Black Church and the Black Family

We are asserting that what has happened in the black family affects what happens in the black church. The church in the black tradition has been an extended family; while the family, in many instances, has been in fact, a "domestic church." Church and family together have nurtured our suffering race and preserved us through all the ordeals of our history.[1]

—J. Deotis Roberts

Who Needs a Balm for Gilead?
Prolegomenon to an Ethic of Pastoral Care for Abused
Black Families

The family and the church are the primary institutions that have nurtured and sustained black communities in the United States since the inception of black families in slavery, their emancipation into freedom, and in their progress toward liberty and justice for all in this country. In the epigraph chosen to set the tone and direction for this chapter, black theologian J. Deotis Roberts clearly highlights the theological and pastoral relationships between the black family and the black church. These relationships are both a means and a viable theological entity in arresting abuse and violence.[2] We believe that the link between the priestly ministry of the black church (its healing, comforting, and succoring work) and its prophetic ministry (involving social justice and socially transforming witness) is the relationship between love and justice. The needs of the black family as a "domestic church" are evident in the refrain from the song, "Balm in Gilead." The song speaks of a healing remedy that we believe is readily available and accessible through the resources of the black church. As the black church strengthens its resources and its public response to the grave and growing problem of domestic abuse and violence rooted in its midst, this balm is amply available.

The traditional, historically documentable response of the black community and of the black church to domestic violence committed against its most vulnerable members—women and children—has been largely one of public silence in the face of a racist and sexist dominant culture. This silence does not stem from acceptance of domestic violence as a black cultural norm (a view that the media perpetuates and many whites believe), but rather from shame, fear, and an understandable, but nonetheless detrimental, sense of racial loyalty. Beth Richie-Bush, former cochair of the National Coalition Against Domestic Violence Women of Color Task Force, has written:

> I gradually realized that some strong, culturally identified families were dangerous places for women to live.... As I began to look closely, the incidence of battering, rape, and sexual harassment became obvious.... Fear of being cast out by the community silenced me in the beginning. Loyalty and devotion are enormous barriers to overcome. Black women be forewarned: there is already so much negative information about our families that a need to protect ourselves keeps us quiet. It is a painful, unsettling task to call attention to violence in our community.[3]

A pernicious combination of internal and external forces has prevented both the black church and the black community from addressing the violence of rape, incest, and domestic violence. Although breaking the silence appears to be dangerous and culturally threatening, it is critical that this silence be broken. It is impossible to build productive communities or strong, loving families if black women and children continue to be the physical and psychological targets of the black community's rage. This problem need not be approached (as perhaps many blacks fear) with finger pointing, cruel accusations, lame excuses, or feelings of betrayal. It can begin, as self-love and liberation historically have for black people, with hazardous but ultimately healing proclamations of truth.

The truth is, of course, that both black men and women are weak, vulnerable, and because of racism, intricately damaged individuals. Black families know that they cannot depend on the police, social workers, or the criminal justice system to protect them from abuse or intervene on their behalf. Often the police department family assistance services have been some of the worst offenders in perpetuating and blatantly ignoring the violence in black communities. And yet, when black families turn to each other to stop the violence in their lives, they are confronted with a myriad of cultural myths, internalized self-hatred, and a pseudotrust in God. Clearly, black family units need to put faith into action and make the commitment to stop hurting and begin trusting and respecting the closest members of our basic social and religious communities.

If indeed this priority is a primary one from the perspectives of multiple black Christian communities, then we must from an African American perspective address this concern about domestic violence rooted within family life. Real insight into the factors that build up or tear down "The Black Family That Is Church"[4] can be achieved only by serious study of the culture, society, and political-economic considerations that envelop and affect this basic social and ecclesial unit.

Such a study must also encompass the religious structures and theological belief systems that surround and support African American families. In exploring aspects of black family life within the context of the black church, consideration will be given in this chapter to two areas: (1) sociotheological perspectives on the black family and (2) a historical review of the meaning of the black church.

This book is dedicated to dealing with the need to provide pastoral care for the very visible and seriously wounded members of the "domestic church" as referred to by J. Deotis Roberts—those African American families who are experiencing and suffering from the incredibly debilitating and diabolical effects engendered by sexual violence and domestic abuse.

Sociotheological Perspectives on the Black Family

African American theologians are increasingly directing their attention to the need for family ministry. Recent black theological attention to sociological literature describing the circumstances of African American families in the United States in terms of crisis began with J. Deotis Roberts' *Roots of a Black Future: Family and Church.*[5] This is a scholarly work aimed at extensively connecting the ethical and classically developed issues of the black family and church. His perceptive and original study traces the historical development of the black church and black families. Roberts relies on a previous but brief treatment of the historical interrelationship between the black family and the black church in a chapter entitled "The Household of Faith" in Olin Moyd's text, *Redemption in Black Theology*. In his text, Moyd highlights the African origin of the black family, reflecting a cultural relativity theory, and seems to prefer the view of W. E. B. DuBois that the church gives shape and form for socialization to the family by being a dominant moral, as well as economic, influence. Moyd offers the black church as a sign of liberation and redemption among black families.

> The Black folks found themselves in a meaningful confederation as they gathered in the church setting. The Black Church was and is the institution which gave meaning to and provided the basic ingredient for family stability. It must be pointed out that in the African tradition the institution of the family is a sacred and a social requirement.... Whatever has gone wrong to mar that African family tradition among American Blacks can definitely be laid to the white oppressors.... But the Black Church served as the redemption center for broken family circles.[6]

J. Deotis Roberts describes the concomitant and coextensive nature of the black family and the black church in its richest and fullest sense as "the experience of *belongingness* of a people"[7] whose cultural, social, and religious identity leads to health, sanity, and wholeness, despite racist oppression. Roberts declares that it is only through the interpenetration of the black family and the black church that socialization and achievement patterns are made most manifest in black people. "It is thus that we discover who we are, and thus that we are able to walk tall in spite of all we must endure."[8]

Through the term "domestic church" as a metaphor for the black family, Roberts has recalled the intimate bond that theologically links family and church in one functional, microcosmic system. Roberts has also established in an extremely precise and yet valuable way that the notion of "family as a domestic church" has its parallels within both the black church traditions and larger ecumenical theology.[9] Roberts succeeded also in coinciding felicitously with renewed Roman Catholic emphasis on family ministry. Although his usage of the phrase antedates the critical papal document, Roberts reinforces the metaphorical refrain emphasized in *Familiaris Consortio: Regarding the Role of the Christian Family in the Modern World*,[10] an apostolic exhortation written by Pope John Paul II. Roberts's main purpose was "to open up important ecclesiological considerations for black theology."[11] However, it must be noted that despite the profound significance of this groundbreaking theological work, there is no mention of domestic violence as either a theological or pastoral issue the black church must address.

Nonetheless, in related work Roberts has continued to urge the black church to become proactive in its ministry to the family, especially with respect to those issues that are germane to the African American condition.[12] He has suggested that this might lead to an investigation of motherhood, a greater respect for responsible fathering, and a more holistic nurturing and development of children. The black church can be particularly helpful in insisting that motherhood, fatherhood, and parenting be studied with an eye on the racist, dominant society in which they consistently arise.

Wallace Charles Smith's *The Church in the Life of the Black Family* [13] is identified as a "pastoral theology" and a "black family theology" that seeks to respond to Roberts's call for black church and theological attention to the social circumstances of African American families.[14] Smith's pastoral reflections consist in developing a family ministry and a call to action that present "the potential for liberation available to blacks through a cooperative effort between churches and families."[15] Despite this positive framework for addressing the African American "domestic church" of the family, Wallace fails to directly deal with the insidious issue of domestic violence.

Smith follows in the direction indicated by Roberts by being attentive to traditional African American and native African resources. Smith is critical of sociological reflections upon the black family because so frequently their conception of family as nuclear in form does not allow for an appreciation of the strengths and virtues of the extended black family's responsiveness to oppressive circumstances.[16] One of the distinctive merits of Smith's analysis is his attention to the status of the elderly in the family, a focus typical of traditional African thinking about family and tribe and those who are increasingly at risk.

Smith has gone so far as to develop a sample curriculum for black family enrichment that is based on four goals: (1) to heighten self-image by the recognition that all persons are created in the image of God; (2) to familiarize African American Christians with resources and methods that enhance family enrichment; (3) to develop skills that foster family enrichment; and (4) to heighten African American Christians' awareness of the problems facing the black family. Smith is convinced that no effective family ministry can take place apart from the recognitions that African Americans, as a whole, compose a suffering and disadvantaged community in the United States.

This reality mandates that family enrichment ministry from the church include a plan for social mobilization designed to help African Americans reach equality with whites in economic development, health care, housing, jobs, and education. The church must fight the historical tendency to concentrate on spiritual development alone. Smith calls for a national effort on the part of the church and proposes a four-pronged attack to family enrichment—preaching, Christian education, counseling, and community organizing.[17] The same kind of emphasis and information must begin to be developed to assist the black church to become a better "balm for Gilead"—better able to heal the potentially fatal wounds inflicted by domestic violence and abuse in its families. The furtherance of this need to heal and the goal of providing pastoral care that is practical and theological are the aims of our text.

Henry H. Mitchell, a preeminent theologian and pastor, and Nicholas Cooper Lewter, a noted pastoral therapist, have identified the home as the best channel through which the black church can provide the "preventative maintenance" of unconditional love and enlightened care.[18] Rather than waiting to aid the person in crisis, they insist that the black church must minister to and in the environment of the home, where many crises originate. This effort to break "the grip of the vicious cycle of the shortage of love" will require a family spiritual discipline similar to the family devotions of an earlier time.[19] In this respect, the black church, which has never lost its identity as an extended family in the context of the African American community, will have to nurture the fractured remnants in order to remake them into an organism of greater trust, love, faith, and shared values. Yet, like Roberts and Wallace, Mitchell and Cooper do not deal directly with the reality of the suffering created by the presence of domestic violence in the confines of the black family.

In addition to theologians, some social scientists are also suggesting ways that the Christian churches in the black community can use a traditional role to enhance the health of African American families. Wade Nobles and Lawford L. Goddard call for the churches to make every effort to influence public policy on behalf of African American families. Among needed reforms they recommend are advocacy for church credit unions, the demand for accurate treatment of African American family life in textbooks and the media, and the demand for an evaluation of the current criminal justice system.

These social scientists also urge the Christian churches to serve as agents of community development by: a link with the business and corporate world in order to generate funds for the community; economic and emotional support for those families that have members in prison; nutrition, education, and food cooperatives; youth employment opportunities; and a forum for the community's discussion of legislative issues that affect the African American community. Finally they suggest that the black church might develop new forms of archives, support computer-based retrieval systems, republish classic works, and support independent research centers.[20] Again, no mention is made of domestic violence and its effects in the black family.

It seems that the church in the black community is beginning to focus on black family life with a new seriousness and vigor. However, domestic violence and abuse are nowhere mentioned as a public issue or concern. Whether or not the pastoral and social service programs and plans we have reviewed will be effective in stemming the tide and the terrors of domestic violence and sexual abuse prevalent in the black community remains to be seen. Regardless, the contemporary and historical black church, as a now very *visible* institution within the context of the black community, continues to operate within a historical paradox. On the one hand, restoration and social services are effectively advocated and in place. On the other hand, social critique and pastoral care on behalf of the victims of sexual abuse and domestic violence are virtually invisible.

The future of the black church as an institution is assured by the existential needs of the African American people. However, unless it decides to develop a more intentional and skilled praxis for ministry that focuses on sexual abuse and domestic violence within it, the black church may well not emerge as a driving force in its social, political, and economic liberation. Renewal of a liberating ministry to the black family that is focused explicitly on reforming and retarding domestic violence and sexual abuse may well be an important primary step toward a revitalized social relevance and, subsequently, a renewed understanding of the black church as a necessary agent in the process of social change.

Documenting the Identity and Advocacy of the Black Church as a Pastoral Change Agent

Because family and church are the two foundational institutions responsible for the nurture, survival, socialization, and secular achievements of black people in this country, there is a need to discuss both familial and church identity within the broader black religious experience in a functional systemic relationship to each other. W. E. B. DuBois, writing around the turn of the century, gave a brilliant and succinct summary of the interrelationship between the role of the black church and the black family:

> The Negro church is the peculiar and characteristic product of the transplanted African.... As a social group, the Negro church may be said to have antedated the Negro family on American soil; as such it has preserved, on the one hand, many functions of tribal organization...and on the other hand, many of the *family* functions. Its tribal functions are shown in its religious activity, its social authority, and general guiding and coordinating work; its *family functions* are shown by the fact that the church is a centre of social life and intercourse.[21]

Although we would take issue with DuBois's point that the black church antedates the black family,[22] we find the argument regarding the primacy of the black church interesting for other reasons, which link the private to the public, or social, understanding of individual membership and its ethical responsibilities to enable pastoral and prophetic activity and advocacy that counters and works toward curing the effects of unabated violence. In the introduction to *The Black Church in America*, Hart Nelsen and his associates have observed,

> It is curious that though it has been argued that the Negro church antedates the Negro family (see, for example,...

DuBois) and that it is generally acknowledged to be, for better or for worse, the center of the black community, the black church has received so little concentrated attention from sociologists. We have found that most texts on sociology of religion or on minority groups give the black church only cursory treatment at best.[23]

Lincoln considers that because of the historically unique nature of the black experience in the United States and because of the centrality of institutionalized religion in the development of that experience, there was an era when the *personal identity* of the black individual was communicated almost entirely through his or her church affiliation.

To be able to say that "I belong to Mt. Nebo Baptist" or "We go to Mason's Chapel Methodist" was the accepted way of establishing identity and status when there were few other criteria by means of which a sense of self or a communication of place could be projected.[24]

In describing the black church by following E. Franklin Frazier's well-known citation in *The Negro Church in America*, C. Eric Lincoln directly connects the unique historic institution of the black church to the broader black community and to its individual membership. Lincoln points out:

To understand the power of the Black Church it must first be understood that there is no disjunction between the Black Church and the Black community. The Church is the spiritual face of the Black community and whether one is a "church member" or not is beside the point in any assessment of the importance and meaning of the Black Church.[25]

Furthermore, in his introduction to *The Black Experience in Religion*, Lincoln continues to define the black church in a way that provides further collective ethical and yet individually responsible references to counter the violence that is decimating black families who may be identified as paradigms of the metaphor established as the "domestic" contemporary expressions of the historic black church:

> The Black Church evolved, not as a formal, black, "denomination," ... but as an attitude, a movement.... It represents the desire of Blacks to be self-conscious about the meaning of their blackness and to search for spiritual fulfillment in terms of their understanding of themselves and their experience of history. The Black [church] then cuts across denominational, cult, and sect lines to do for black people what other religions have not done: to assume the black man's humanity, his responsibility, his participation, and his right to see himself as the image of God.[26]

This term, *black church,* came into vogue when *black* began to connote ethnic pride, affirmation of the history and culture of African Americans, and solidarity and militancy in the struggle against all forms of white domination and racism. Applied to the religious and social institution of church then, *blackness* meant the renewal and enhancement of the most esteemed values of African American spirituality, the search for distinctive norms and characteristics of African and African American religion, and the refusal to accept European American theology and church structures as the only norms for operation and organization.[27]

Daniel C. Thompson, in the *Sociology of the Black Experience,* offers yet another view of the nexus between the black family and the black church, one which fosters socialization and achievement patterns for black people who have, and who offer in their pastoral praxis patterns, a developing concern for the establishment of a more realistic "balm for Gilead."

> Since perennially the Black community has been powerless, next to the family the Black church has had the greatest

influence in the social, cultural, and psychological matura-
tion of Blacks. Even now, it is the only truly powerful
national organization, including Blacks on all socioeconomic levels.[28]

Obviously, there is a tremendous need to continue to
define and to discuss family and church in the black experience together since there is also a clear gap in sociological
and theological literature on the topic. Only one sociologist, Robert Staples, has made a comprehensive effort to
relate these two institutional concerns in his *Introduction to
Black Sociology.* His book clearly offers a much less glowing
outlook on the role and function of the black church for the
black family.[29] Although Staples's perspective may convey
a negative overall impression, his work is somewhat
unique in light of the comment by Hart Nelsen, cited earlier, that sociologists rarely give significant attention to the
black church.

Applying elements of the structural-functionalist sociological approach to black religion, Staples takes particular
care to note some latent functions of the institution of the
black church for the black family: like churches in most
societies, the black church often stands as a steward of
morals, a strengthener of family life, and as a final authority on right and wrong.[30] In its socialization role the black
church encouraged the establishment of the monogamic
family and urged black men to become more diligent
providers for their wives and children. Nonetheless,
Staples chooses to defer in the end of his assessment to
John Scanzoni's study, *The Black Family in Modern Society,* in
order to draw his conclusive links between the black family and the black church.

Scanzoni found in his study of "stable" black families
that the majority of the respondents had parents who
attended church at least once a week. Consequently the
link he saw between the black family and religion was the

transmittal and reinforcement of values leading to optimum fulfillment of dominant expectations regarding economic and conjugal behavior.

Our overarching theory is that the black church has the potential and residual power from God for renewing and deepening its abiding identity as a "balm for Gilead." With so many suffering black families who are models of the "domestic church," we too are sustained by the wisdom of a perennially soothing biblical resource contained in the song:

> There is a balm in Gilead, to make the wounded whole,
> There is a balm in Gilead, to heal the sin-sick soul.
>
> Sometimes I feel discouraged, and think my work's in
>   vain,
> But then the Holy Spirit revives my soul again.
>
> Don't ever feel discouraged, for Jesus is your friend,
> And if you look for knowledge, He'll ne'er refuse to lend.
>
> If you cannot preach like Peter, if you cannot pray like Paul,
> You can tell the love of Jesus, and say "He died for all."
>
> There is a balm in Gilead, to make the wounded whole,
> There is a balm in Gilead, to heal the sin-sick soul.[31]

CHAPTER TWO

The Context of Oppression and Abuse for African American Families

The slave system in the United States was especially vicious in regard to family life. The family was broken up at the very beginning of the slave trade in the manner...[of] disregard the captors showed for family and kinship ties.... Slave women were exploited by white owners...for pleasure and profit. A role for the black man as husband and father was systematically denied.... In a word, the black family had no physical, psychological, social, or economic protection. This crippled individuals, families—a whole people. The "lengthening shadow of slavery" still hovers over the black family. We shall not be able to correct this until the cause behind the present plight of the black family is recognized.[1]

Racism as the Genesis of Systemic Abuse and Oppression in African American Families

Though it may sound like an overworked and now meaningless cliché, the wholesale destruction of the black family began during slavery.[2] Whites, in order to maintain the slave system and to justify their inhuman treatment of blacks, developed a vicious mythology to support their actions. To the detriment of all society, this mythology persists to this day. White people based their barbaric system of supremacy, domination, and control on the belief that all black people were insatiable sexual beasts.[3]

This attitude served several purposes: (1) it "legitimized" fear among whites, giving them reason to use whatever method of cruelty (the whipping post, auction block, or lynch mob) they deemed necessary to control the "ravenous" impulses of blacks;[4] (2) it sanctioned the sexual exploitation of black women by white men and fueled the myth that black women are promiscuous and immoral;[5] (3) it deified the white woman, making her the consummate symbol of goodness, beauty, virginity and purity, who was *not* to be defiled;[6] and (4) it completely terrorized black families, for a black man accused of even thinking sexual thoughts about a white woman would be hung without question from the most convenient tree.

These brutally racist attitudes gave whites the means to control the thoughts and actions of black people. It licensed them to destroy black families, rape black women, and kill black men. Racism extolled the virtues of everything that is white and reduced blackness and an entire race of people to animal savagery. During slavery white people taught themselves to despise and fear blacks. It is a lesson they learned well. Blacks learned perseverance, faith, creativity, but also hopelessness, despair, powerlessness, and defeat in the face of never-ending white oppression. Racism taught black people hatred, lack of confidence, mistrust, and disdain for themselves.

The experience of slavery, in conjunction with these sentiments, provides fertile ground for the expectation and tolerance of violence in black lives. An African legacy, now being re-remembered and reclaimed by many local black churches who are deliberately and intentionally seeking Afrocentric styles of worship, leadership, and congregational education, is becoming a counterbalance for the violence and the abuse experienced by the interiorization and internalization of racism and self-hatred within black families and individuals.

An African Legacy

According to many scholars, there is an African legacy operative within African American families. In spite of attempts during slavery to destroy all vestiges of African culture among the slaves, certain patterns seem to be clearly preserved and, in fact, have been crucial to the survival of a people. Renowned African American family therapist Nancy Boyd-Franklin asserts that two indispensable aspects are:

> The concept of family kinship and collective unity and...the role of religion and the African philosophy of life.... The legacy of this belief system has survived years of slavery and has influenced both the strong sense of "family" (i.e., the extended family group) and the very strong religious or spiritual orientation of many Black Afro-American families today.[7]

The African tribe functioned as an extended family in which the individual was not clearly distinct from the group, and personal and corporate identity tended to merge.

> Traditional African family life was patriarchal, polygynous, communal, tribal, and organized around elaborate kinship ties.... It was not disorganized and lacking in civilization as generally perceived by many Americans. Even though there was constant friction between different African tribes, intratribal life gave tribal members a strong sense of family and community. Their lives were oriented around the life of their tribe. Their identity could not be seen as separate from the customs of tribal life.[8]

The extended family remains the primary social unit in the African American community. Persons tend to be bonded to one another in extended groups that do not correspond to the nuclear family, and the support network functions as a unit for survival and enjoyment.

> When we speak of a black extended family, we mean a multigenerational, interdependent kinship system which is welded together by a sense of obligation to relatives; is organized around a "family base" household; is generally guided by a "dominant family figure"; extends across geographical boundaries to connect family units to an extended family network; and has a built-in mutual aid system for the welfare of its members and the maintenance of the family as a whole.[9]

In African society, religion was not just an aspect of life but a comprehensive system that influenced everything. Good and evil spirits were everywhere and made up a religious outlook on all of life.

> As to religion, the natives believe that there is one Creator of all things, and that he lives in the sun, and is girded round with a belt, that he may never eat or drink; but according to some, he smokes a pipe, which is our favorite luxury. They believe he governs events, especially our deaths or captivity; but as for the doctrine of eternity, I do not remember to have ever heard of it: some however believe in the transmigration of souls in a certain degree. Those spirits, which are not transmigrated, such as their dear friends or relations, they believe always attend them, and guard them from the bad spirits of their foes.[10]

This excerpt is typical of some of the early historical summaries of African religious beliefs which were continued by the slaves in the New World. One of the most popular beliefs was in *Obeah*, a belief that certain spiritual leaders can influence the daily lives of people.[11] This belief is based on the worldview that spirits are omnipresent and awareness of their reality is crucial to human survival and happiness. The tendency of white Christians to dismiss such a religious worldview as pagan and mere superstition was one of the forms of genocide aimed at the African culture.[12]

Despite the suppression of African religions in the United States, aspects of the African worldview have persisted and give energy to the Christian, Islamic, and other religious traditions in which African American families participate. The major characteristics of the various black churches today contain forms of spirituality that seem to be consistent with certain African patterns, such as the emphasis on the welfare of the black community and on holistic religion that involves all of experience, including the emotions.

> The black sacred cosmos of the religious world view of African Americans is related both to their African heritage, which envisaged the whole universe as sacred, and to their conversion to Christianity during slavery and its aftermath.... The core values of black culture like freedom, justice, equality, an African heritage, and racial parity at all levels of human intercourse, are raised to ultimate levels and legitimated by the black sacred cosmos.[13]

Afrocentric values and rituals are being integrated into African American churches, families, and other institutions in the black community. Examples of such formal and informal values and rituals are the bestowing and taking of African names for children and by family members, the practice of "rites of passage" for adolescent boys and girls that were incorporated into the now classic film version of *Roots* by Alex Haley, and marriage rituals such as "jumping the broomstick" and "marrying in blankets" (the practice of giving or displaying inherited or reconstructed Afrocentric quilts as wedding presents or as symbols of the marriage covenant).

—— 39 ——

The Impact of Racism, Sexism, and Classism on the Ongoing Formation of the Black Family

The story of African American families during slavery displays a careful balancing between the consequences of this dehumanizing and genocidal system and amazing resilience of the extended families and their religious beliefs. This balance has not always been kept by some writers, and thus, scholarship tended to contribute to continuing racism by blaming the family for the effects of slavery. "[Some sociologists] did not misperceive the oppressive nature of enslavement but underestimated the adaptive capacities of the enslaved and those born to them and to their children."[14]

> The institution of slavery was disruptive by nature: Slave masters attempted to destroy the kinship bonds and the cultural system of Black Africans.... Despite the attempts to deprive them of any form of human rights and of their own culture, Black people sought to maintain family tribal customs and spiritual rituals. There are many examples of this survival of human dignity in the face of enforced degradation. Black people created their own marriage rituals such as "jumping the broom," which acknowledged a union between a man and a women. The process of informal adoption had its origins in African tribal traditions and in the "taking in" of children by other slave families when their parents were sold or killed. Spirituality survived in many forms, most saliently in an African belief in familial and tribal reunion in the afterlife.[15]

Racism and Discrimination

The end of slavery did not initiate the process of full citizenship for African Americans. Instead, a network of formal and informal restrictions and violence continued in both North and South to limit the resources and potential of persons of African descent. Discrimination based on national origin and skin color became a central organizing principle of American culture, economics, and politics with the resultant marginalization and deprivation. Again, the incredible resilience of many families is a testimony to the ability of the human spirit to resist even overwhelming evil.

> It is difficult to convey fully to someone who has not experienced it the insidious, pervasive, and constant impact that racism and discrimination have on the lives of Black people in America today. Both affect a Black person from birth until death and have an impact on every aspect of family life, from child-rearing practices, courtship, and marriage, to male-female roles, self-esteem, and cultural and racial identification. They also influence the way in which Black people relate to each other and to the outside world.
>
> Slavery set the tone for Black people to be treated as inferior. Skin color was and is a badge of difference. The process of discrimination is evident at all levels of society from theories about genetic inferiority and cultural pathology to segregation that existed blatantly in the South until the Civil Rights era in the 1960s and still occurs in subtler forms today. There are continued inequities in the United States...that are manifested by the disproportionate numbers of Black people who are poor, homeless, living in substandard housing, unemployed, and school dropouts.[16]

Racism and Sexism[17]

Racism and sexism are the two primary negative factors that affect the family and interpersonal relationships between black women and black men. Any ethical or theological reflection on the issue of racism in relation to sexism requires a coming to terms with the suffering and oppression that have marked past pathological relationships between black women and black men. Honest reflection on the issue of sexism in relation to racism may also highlight positive aspects of the challenge and conversion available to black and believing women and men who want to deal with their own spirituality and sexuality as a means of coming to terms with a new family life in God.

Womanist theologian Jacquelyn Grant explains the effects of sexual dualism on the self-image of black people. "Racism and sexism are interrelated," she says, "just as all forms of oppression are interrelated."[18] Racism and sexism have provided a theological problem within the Christian community composed of both black women and men who theoretically are equally concerned about the presence of freedom and justice for all.

> Sexism, however, has a reality of its own because it represents that peculiar form of oppression suffered by Black women at the hands of Black men. It is important to examine this reality of sexism as it operated in both the Black Community and the Black Church.[19]

A careful diagnosis of the sickness and the sin of sexism within the black church calls forth a challenge to clergy and laity alike. The failure of the black church and of black theology itself to proclaim explicitly the liberation of black women and all others who experience violence and abuse within the confines of the black family, which is the domestic church, indicates, according to this assessment, that neither black theology nor the black church can unequivocally claim to be an agent of divine liberation or of the God whom the evangelist describes as the Author and Exemplar of black love. If black theology, like the black church, has no clear and definitive word for black women and others who experience violence and abuse in its diverse forms, particularly within the context of the family, then its conception of liberation is unauthentic and dysfunctional.

Sexism aggravated by racism takes two basic forms in black male-female relationships: sexist and spiritualistic splits (divisions within reality).[20]

1. *Sexist dualism* refers to the systematic subordination of black women in church and society, within interpersonal relationships between males and females, as well as within linguistic patterns and thought formulations by which women are dominated. Hence the term "patriarchal dualism" may be also appropriate, or more simply, the contemporary designation of "sexism," may be used.

2. *Spiritualistic dualism* has its roots in the body-spirit dichotomy abounding in white, Western philosophy and culture introduced at the beginning of the Christian era. (Hence, the term "Hellenistic dualism" is also appropriate.) It must be noted in offering these descriptive distinctions about sexist and spiritual dualisms that African philosophy and culture were and still are significantly different from these white, Western conceptualizations.[21] It is this African worldview, held by African familial, clan, and tribal groupings, that has given rise to the holistic potential residing in authentic expressions of African American familial spirituality and sexuality today.

Sexist dualism has not only pathologically scarred the white community from which it originated but has also had its negative effect within the black family, which we have been identifying as the domestic church, as well as within the larger religious and secular communities in which black people reside and survive. Sexist dualism, which has been organized along racial lines, refers to "schizophrenic" male attitudes toward women in general, who are imaged as either the virgin or the whore—the polemical Mary or Eve archetype represented by the female gender.[22] The prevailing model of beauty in the white, male-dominated American society has been the "long-haired blond" with all that accompanies this mystique. Because of this worldview, black women have had an additional problem with this false ideal as they encounter black men who have appropriated this norm as their own.

Sexist, as well as racist, dualisms have elevated the image of the white woman, in accordance with the requirements of a white worldview, into the respected symbol of femininity and purity while the black woman must represent an animality, which can be ruthlessly exploited for both sex and labor. Similarly, the sexist dualism present within pseudobiblical teaching argues that *woman* is responsible for the Fall of "*man*kind" and is, consequently, the source of sexual evil. This dualistic doctrine has had its doubly detrimental effect in the experience of many black women.[23] The self-image and self-respect of many black women is dealt a double blow by both black religion and black society. Thus, black women are made to believe, or at least accept on the surface, that they are evil, ugly, insignificant, and the underlying source of trouble, especially when the sense of intimacy begins to break down in black love and familial relationships.

This dualistic doctrine has nurtured a kind of compensatory black male chauvinism (as evidenced in typical black church patterns and black nationalism movements) in order to restore the "manliness" of the one who had traditionally been humiliated by being deprived (according to a white patriarchal model) of being the primary protector of his family. In this manner, sexist dualism has been a central limitation in the development of a black love, which at its zenith is the most authentic expression we have of the unity of black spirituality and sexuality as it must be expressed within the diverse forms of the black family.

A disembodied spirituality has also been a central limitation in the development of black love. Spiritualistic dualism has been a central factor in persistent efforts to portray faithful black love as an unfashionable and hopelessly anachronistic way of establishing black liberation and black material achievement.

Eldridge Cleaver obviously recognized the racism and sexism in this spiritualistic form of dualism. Cleaver readily identified bodily scapegoating as an aspect of the sickness within racist/sexist relationships: "Only when the white man comes to respect his own body, to accept it as part of himself will he be able to accept the black man's mind and treat him as something other than the living symbol of what he has rejected in himself."[24] Bodily scapegoating implies a discomfort with our own bodies that leads us to discredit any human body-person who differs too much from the appearance of our own bodies. This scapegoating is particularly evident in racist, white-black relationships. But it is equally obvious in the revealing and discrediting attitudes of some men, white and black, about the assumed menstrual "uncleanness" of women or the intrinsic "repulsiveness" of the pregnant female form.

Because blackness has long been understood as a symbol for filth as well as evil, a spiritualistic dualism prevalent in the worldview of many white people has allowed them the racist option of projecting onto black persons any dirty or disgusting bodily feelings that they may harbor within themselves. Because of the fertility potential symbolized by the female menstrual and pregnancy cycles, spiritualistic and sexist dualism has also been created and sustained by some white and black males, which has allowed them to act out their own latent anxieties and hostilities by sexually depreciating—primarily by violent, destructive, and degrading actions—the value and worth of the black female person.[25]

As long as we feel insecure as human beings about our bodies, we will very likely be anxious or hostile about other body-persons who are obviously racially or sexually different from our own embodied selves. Thus, the most dehumanizing spoken expressions of hostility or overt violence within racist and/or sexist experiences are often linked with depreciating the body or body functions of someone else. Worse yet, the greatest dehumanization or violence that actually can occur in racist and/or sexist situations happens when persons of the rejected racial- or gender-specific group begin to internalize the judgments made by others and become convinced of their own personal inferiority. Obviously, the most affected and, thus, dehumanized victims of this experience are black women.

Racism and sexism diminish the ability of black families, and within this context the abilities of women and men, to establish relationships of mutuality, integrity, and trust. Racism and sexism undermine the black communities in which black people live, pray, and work out their salvation in the sight of God and one another. However, in coming to terms with racism and sexism as oppressions affecting us all, the black church does have access to the black family and community in ways that many other institutions do not. The black church has a greater potential to achieve both liberation and reconciliation by attending carefully to the relationships that have been weakened between black males and females, and within the family structures themselves.

Because the black church has access, and is often indeed the presiding and official agent in the process of sexual socialization for black families, it has a potentially unlimited opportunity to restore the ancient covenant of Scripture and tradition, which upholds the beauty of black love in its most profound meaning. Wherever black love is discouraged or disparaged as an unfashionable or unattainable expression between black women and black men, the black church has an unparalleled option to model these gospel values of love and unconditional acceptance. By offering from its storehouse an authentic understanding of black spirituality and sexuality, the black church becomes paradigmatic of the reign of God materializing and entering into our midst.

Racism and Classism

According to the 1980 census, black children accounted for about 15 percent of all children in the United States. From 1976 to 1980, the proportion of child abuse and neglect reports involving black children remained fairly constant at about 19 percent, but national data for 1982 showed that black children were the victims in 22 percent of all child maltreatment reports. In 1984, black children accounted for 20.8 percent of Child Protective Services (CPS) cases.[26] These figures seem to confirm the conclusion that "black Americans as a group are considered more violent than white Americans."[27] However, these figures do not prove that child abuse correlates with race. Statistics about abuse need to be correlated with socioeconomic situations. There is some evidence that black children in families in extreme poverty fare better than white children in extreme poverty because of survival mechanisms such as the extended family.[28]

Some scholars suggest that research must be done to correlate abuse with the status of local communities, whether they are stable or fragmented, whether they have a history of coping with problems or are besieged and overwhelmed. Another factor is whether the reporting systems include any bias such that "children from poor and minority families are more vulnerable to receiving the label 'abused' than children from more affluent households, who are more likely to be classified as victims of accidents."[29] Some research shows that recognition of child abuse by physicians was affected by the severity of the child's injury and by the parents' socioeconomic status and ethnicity.[30]

The topic of abuse within African American families is controversial because of distortions in theories and research methods by the dominant European American society. Most research on family violence does not carefully sort out race, socioeconomic status, and other cultural variables.[31] When crude measurements are made, the prevalence of family violence within African American families appears to be higher than in the white population. This unscientific approach has been used to justify the politicization of this issue and the adoption of oppressive public policies toward African American families.

Black families and single parents have been blamed for the poverty of the inner cities in order to avoid political responsibility for structural poverty. It is important to carefully review this discussion before trying to understand the dynamics of family violence. Robert Hampton, a premier researcher on violence among African American families, offers as an example what is commonly taken for granted, that Americans, as a group, are more violent than people of any other developed country in the world. He notes a stereotype often prevalent in the dominant and black cultures, that black Americans, as a group, are more violent than white Americans.[32]

However, there is a vigorous discussion among African American social scientists about the validity of these kinds of stereotypes and statements.

> When class and ethnicity are confounded, we always run the risk of confusing legitimate ethnic differences in style with the deleterious effects of socioeconomic deprivation... and of elevating the values of the economic privileged to the status of universal standards.[33]

There is a tendency to search for a single factor that explains the prevalence of violence in black families. One such attempt is the "subculture of violence thesis," which "argues that certain segments of society have adopted distinctively violent subcultural values."[34] This argument suggests that because of African values and the impact of slavery and discrimination, cheapness of life and brutality have become ingrained in the African American subculture, resulting in a "lack of regard for sacredness of life."[35]

Another attempt to find a single factor to explain the prevalence of violence in black families is the debate about the so-called dysfunctional black family.

> The notorious 1965 government study on the "Negro Family"—popularly known as the "Moynihan Report"—directly linked the contemporary social and economic problems of the Black community to a putatively matriarchal family structure.... According to the report's thesis, the source of oppression was deeper than the racial discrimination that produced unemployment, shoddy housing, inadequate education and substandard medical care. The root of oppression was described as a "tangle of pathology" created by the absence of male authority among Black people! The controversial finale of the Moynihan Report was a call to introduce male authority (meaning male supremacy of course!) into the Black family and the community at large.[36]

In the 1992 State of the Union Address, President George Bush said that *the* cause of urban poverty is the collapse of the family. Other commentators have expanded this to mean that the black, single parent family with its violence and inability to socialize children is the single cause of the persistence of poverty in the African American community.

> Dr. Martin Luther King's critique of the original Moynihan Report, in which he called attention to the danger that "problems will be attributed to innate Negro weaknesses and used to justify neglect and rationalize oppression" is no less relevant [today].[37]

Rejecting such single-factor analyses, African American social scientists suggest that understanding the African American family within its social context, including the prevalence of violence, requires an ecological, multifactor theory. This model would examine not only race, subculture, and socioeconomic factors but also other variables, such as macroanalysis of economic and political history and analysis of "environmental (neighborhood or community) quality...[and] the cultural, economic, and demographic factors that shape the quality of life for families."[38]

For example, the rates of family violence might be different in a stable, homogeneous black community, even if it is poor, than in a transient, fragmented community that is besieged by police surveillance. This would mean that a multifactor analysis would reveal more valid sources of violence than racial subculture or single parent families as single-factor explanations. An example of such an ecological model for understanding the African American family is presented by James P. Comer in his trenchant commentary included in *American Violence and Public Policy.*[39] Comer observes:

> Americans regularly think of crime and violence as willful, even sinful, bad behavior that will yield only to punishment. This attitude is seductive, because crime and violence are often, as an end product, the consequence of deliberate acts. But such acts are, at the same time, the consequence of a complex social process that involves more than the individual.... [A] perspective is needed that takes into account the complex way in which multiple factors interact to adversely affect particular individuals, families, and their social networks or groups. The perspective must include a consideration of historical, present, and future interactions among families, their primary social network and the larger society.... The perspective must also include the peculiar ability of the human individual not to be affected in a predictable way by family and social network conditions.[40]

The Context of Oppression and Abuse for African American Families

In *The Third Life of Grange Copeland*, Pulitzer Prize-winning author Alice Walker writes with eloquent, insightful passion about the devastating effects of racism and self-hatred on a Southern black family. She explains, but by no means excuses, the violent actions that black men direct toward black women—the individuals least responsible for what they have suffered in American society.

> His crushed pride, his battered ego, made him drag Mem away from school teaching. Her knowledge reflected badly on a husband who could scarcely read and write. It was his great ignorance that sent her into white homes as a domestic, his need to bring her down to his level! It was his rage at himself, and his life and his world that made him beat her for an imaginary attraction she aroused in other men, crackers, although she was no party to any of it. His rage and his anger and his frustration ruled. His rage could and did blame everything, everything on her.[41]

Compassionate and truthful words such as these and the mockingly and ironically humorous, but "deadly" serious, verse of a poet like Pat Parker—

> Brother
> I don't want to hear
> about
> how *my* real enemy
> is the system.
> i'm no genius
> but i do know
> that system
> you hit me with
> is called
> a fist.[42]

—are needed to move beyond our victimized, self-pitying status and make black people take responsibility for what transpires within our families. Black men will not heal their wounded pride or regain a sense of dignity by exerting violent, totalitarian rule over black women. Contrary to the popular black matriarch myth, black women have never had the power or the desire to take the black man's dignity away. Because of awareness of the systematic oppression of black men through lynchings, imprisonment, unemployment, and the sexual politics of the ever-prevalent "rape" charge, black women have, if anything, been forgiving, accepting, and infinitely understanding of words and actions that have ultimately hurt them.

Black women, in the varied names of compassion, religion, or "strong, black womanhood," have allowed black men to treat them as though they (and not a white racist culture) are the worst enemy of black masculinity. And for this physical and emotional sacrifice, have black women received understanding or comfort for their pains? Have black children learned sensitivity or tenderness from the black male figures in their lives? More often than not, it would seem, forgiveness has been met with stronger blows and more debilitating insults. And what is most distressing is that many black women have come to believe that they deserve such treatment and are "strong" enough to bear the pain.

In light of the development of themes of racist, sexist, classist oppression and its impact on the African American family, it is not difficult to generalize initial responses to the following questions often posed by abused black women and children. Where did this abusive behavior come from? Why was the family secretive about what happened, and why did they refuse to seek the help that vulnerable family members needed? Why was the black church, to which many abused women and children belong, silent on the existence of such evil? Where were the schools and other agencies concerned with abused children when these black family members faced their trauma? Why were these symptoms overlooked?

However, we know well, to our abiding discontent, that there are no simple answers to these questions. In an individualistic society, there is a tendency to blame individuals for such destructiveness and violence. Often the victim is blamed for provoking such behavior or for being unable to forget and live as if nothing happened. Sometimes the perpetrator is blamed as if social attitudes about sexuality, violence, race, class, and gender had no bearing on the behavior of persons. While there is plenty of room for individual responsibility in situations such as these, our aim is to understand why such violations of the human spirit are so frequent and widespread and how to prevent them so that victims of violence and abuse are safe and perpetrators are held accountable.

CHAPTER THREE

Defining Abuse in African American Families

Undoubtedly, the stress black men endure is cruel and often overwhelming. The connection this has to black women accepting beatings puzzles me.... Black Women, be forewarned. It is a painful, unsettling task to call attention to violence in our community.... There is already so much negative information about our families that a need to protect ourselves keeps us quiet. Yet we must not allow our voices to be silenced. Instead we must speak the truths about our families; we must support each other; but we must hear the cries of our battered sisters and let them be heard by others.[1]

In order to understand abuse, we must turn again to the difficulties of research on black families. There have been virtually no sustained, social scientific studies of violence in black families. Of three textbooks that purport to be comprehensive, none treats ethnicity, race, or culture as important variables in studying family violence.[2] Only one extensive volume tries to understand violence in black families, and it relies on inadequate research.[3]

Although the media and the public have shown an increasing interest in child maltreatment in recent years, relatively little attention has been given to violence against black children. The few studies that have examined child abuse and neglect in black families have done so only in passing. Few researchers have attempted to develop a more precise conceptual or empirical understanding of the nature, type, and severity of family violence experienced by black children.[4]

Extended and scholarly resources on coping with violence from the perspective and experience of black women are beginning to appear.[5] *Crossing the Boundary: Black Women Survive Incest* by Melba Wilson is an excellent resource. In this text, Wilson asks the most crucial questions in regard to black women and sexual abuse: Where is the community? In the fear and pain of harassment and physical attack, where is the support black women might naturally expect from their families? How far will some members of the family go to deny and cover up the mistreatment of black women? Wilson follows a very complex path that is both deeply personal and highly professional, and however tough the questions, she makes it clear that they must be answered ultimately by the women and children who have survived, as well as by those who identify themselves as members of the black community. However, she does not raise questions related to the presence, role, and responsibility of the black church.

Evelyn C. White sheds some perspective on why this may be the case:

> As with the issues of rape, incest, homosexuality, and alcoholism, clergy members are only beginning to receive adequate training on domestic violence. It is only in the past decade or so that many of these issues have lost their social stigmas. Because black women usually comprise seventy percent of any black congregation, it is perhaps more regrettable, but not surprising that the black clergy has been as uninformed about the extent and severity of domestic violence as anyone else.[6]

We have already noted that there is a perception among some that black families are more violent than other families in the United States.[7] This perception affects public and political debates and decisions about the allocation of resources. The recent dramatic cuts in support for families living in poverty have been partially justified on the basis of a perception of black violence.[8] Perceptions of black violence have been crucial in the public mind as a justification for this state of affairs. This means that the need for research to understand violence in black families is urgent. Some scholars are making valiant efforts to correct this deficiency, but credible research takes time.

Given the absence of reliable facts about violence in black families, and the urgency of some discussion about this topic, this chapter attempts to bring the wisdom from the general debate about family violence into dialogue with the discussion by black scholars about the nature of African American families. We hope that our attempt to bridge these fields will contribute to the effort to begin to understand the causes and consequences of abuse within the African American context until more research can be done.[9]

The Strengths of African American Families

The importance of identifying strengths of African American families at the beginning of this chapter is to counteract the destructive and untrue racist myths, which dominate public perception in both white and black communities.

> The myths...are familiar to all: that the black family is "matriarchal," it is unstable, it does not prepare black people for productive lives, and it is the prime source of black economic weakness.... Readers will find, instead, what black people have known all along: that despite tremendous odds, the black family has been a bulwark of black achievement, that it has proved a flexible and adaptable instrument for black survival, and that it has been the nourishing foundation of positive aspects of the black experience.... I hope the malicious game of blaming the black family for the results of discrimination and oppression will be ended.[10]

In order to discuss the reality of abuse within black families, we must free ourselves of these myths and reject the stereotypes that identify any variation from the nuclear, male-dominated, white, middle-class family as pathological. Various forms of abuse do exist in black families, as they do in all ethnic groups, and this abuse must be addressed honestly and courageously. But it must be done within a context of sensitivity to the history and adaptive structures of the families we are concerned about. One way to do this is to identify the strengths of black families.

> The focus on strengths in terms of Black family life-styles began in the late 1960s. Hill cites strong kinship bonds, strong work orientation, adaptability of family roles, high achievement orientation, and strong religious orientation as important strengths of the Black families he studied.[11]

Robert Hill analyzed and summarized the relevant research. When studied within the context of racism, sexism, and poverty, the majority of black families prove to be cohesive, adaptive, work and achievement oriented, and religious. We will adopt this framework as one part of the dialogue with the emerging literature about the nature of abuse within families. A parallel development in more recent years has been the focus on the Afrocentric value system, *Nguzo Saba,* established by Dr. Ron Karanga and summarized here by a group of sixth-grade students:

> UMOJA...UNITY: We can work and play together. We must work with the people in our family and in our school and in the community of African American people.
>
> KUJICHAGULIA...SELF-DETERMINATION: It seems hard to say, but I try and try to learn it, and learn that it's about making up my mind to "keep on keeping on" in everything I do.

UJIMA...COLLECTIVE WORK AND RESPONSIBILITY: Shared work is team work. You help me and I help you...If you have a problem, you can lean on me...When I have a problem you are able to help me.

UJAMAA...COOPERATIVE ECONOMICS: One person alone may not have a lot; but when each person puts in her share of work, wealth and will-power, everybody has more.

NIA...PURPOSE: I want a good home and a good school and a good community. I will make a plan every day so I will know what to do to make the good things happen.

KUUMBA...CREATIVITY: I create plans for a good home and a good school and a good community...I can create beautiful things, and I will, because inside I am a beautiful person.

IMANI...FAITH: I believe that sharing together is good. I believe that making up my own mind and sticking to it is good too...I believe that planning and doing the right things is good. All these things help make me beautiful inside. I believe they will help me see the beautiful old people and the little babies that will come in the future.[12]

One way to understand abuse is that it violates the historical values of black families and the Afrocentric values that are the strength of the African American community.

What Is Abuse for African American Families?

Defining Abuse

Abuse can be defined as any behavior or pattern of behavior, by a person (or persons) with power, that is judged by a mixture of cultural and community values and professional expertise to be inappropriate and damaging.[13]

The principles of this definition, we believe, can be applied to many forms of violence in African American families, such as violence toward women, toward children, between spouses, between siblings, toward elderly persons, and so on. The strength of this definition is that it is specific to both culture and community values and that it is open to change as values evolve. Abuse expressed within the African American family can be understood as the behavior of a person in power or authority (such as a parent, spouse, community leader, or someone stronger) toward someone dependent or otherwise subject to the behavior of the other.

Such behavior must be judged both inappropriate for black culture and community and damaging to the victim, as determined by general community norms and discussion of such issues by a professional community (especially in technological, urban societies such as the United States). When black cultural and community attitudes, professional experts, and victims agree that a pattern of behaviors is inappropriate and damaging, then it is deemed abusive. With regard to African American families, this means attending to the community values and perspectives rather than uncritically accepting the views of the dominant culture.

Central to this understanding of abuse present within the black family is the exercise of power.[14] In order to be abused, a victim must be in a position where some sort of power (physical, psychological, social, political) can be used for another's benefit or detriment. Since all persons are in relationships to others who can make decisions for their benefit or detriment, abuse of power is a potential danger for everyone. In the black family, there are different degrees of power: parents over children; men over women; older over younger; those physically stronger over those less strong; physically and mentally abled over those differently, physically and mentally abled; and so forth.

Wherever there is power difference, there is potential for power to be used constructively or destructively.

Abuse of power highlights the wish to control another, which is often a primary motive for behaviors that are judged abusive. Physical, sexual, or emotional abuse always serves the needs of perpetrators rather than victims. It is behavior designed to benefit the abuser rather than the one forced to submit to what is demanded. Sometimes the motive is gratification of impulses, such as sexual gratification or discharge of rage and aggression. At other times the motive is punishment for acts of autonomy or independence and an attempt to control the other.[15]

Abuse of power is clearly a part of the dynamic of racism in the United States. Because of norms that favor persons of European descent, and because of inequality of resources, white Americans directly and indirectly behave in destructive ways toward African Americans. Sometimes such behavior is directly racist, such as terrorist activities of the White Citizens Council and other white supremacist organizations. At other times, the abuse of power is exercised by discrimination in matters such as housing, jobs, education, and other resources crucial for participation in American society. When access to resources is made dependent on already having resources, such as money, education, and job experience, then abuse of power can easily result. The racism in the United States is abuse of power by European Americans over African Americans and other persons of color.[16]

Abuse of power expressed within the black family is often a result of the inequality between men and women. In patriarchal, American society, even though the broader black culture is often seen as more egalitarian, traditionally within the black church men's and women's roles are defined as complementary and hierarchical.[17] Black men are often expected to provide major physical resources for the family, such as money, housing, protection, and other instrumental needs. Black women are expected to provide emotional resources for the family, such as nurture and encouragement for the children and comfort and sexual response to the husband.[18] Variations from this nuclear, male-dominated, and more culturally dominant model of the family are often treated with disdain and discrimination.[19] Single parent families headed by women experience poverty at a rate double that of two-parent families. The extended family and informal adoption patterns in the African American community are judged dysfunctional, and punitive public policies bring the poverty rate for black children to over 40 percent. Such policies illustrate an abuse of power that is both racist and sexist.[20]

Within African American families, abuse of power is usually a combination of the authority of parents over children, the dominance of men over women, and the social conditions that create stress and inequalities in the black family. Some forms of abuse are clearly the misuse of parental authority. Women more often engage in the physical abuse of young black children since they are the primary caregivers for this age group. But men perpetuate the majority of physical, sexual, and emotional abuse of black women and older children. Abusive men use the dominant position granted by the society to exercise power that is destructive to others. Thus, violence in the African American family is often organized by gender, that is, the dominance of men over women and children.[21]

Abusive Behaviors Present in African American Families

Given this understanding of the nature of abuse, we can now begin to identify the specific behaviors that are involved in abuse.[22] One of the major characteristics of such a list is that no healthy person would voluntarily choose to be the victim of such behaviors, though their use by persons in power is commonly rationalized and justified.

Physical Abuse
- to hit, slap, punch, shove, bite, cut, choke, kick, burn, or spit
- to throw objects at or restrain another
- to threaten to hurt with an object or deadly weapon (a gun, knife, baseball bat, brick, chain, hammer, scissors, rope, belt buckle, extension cord, branch, bottle, acid, bleach, or scalding water)
- to abandon or lock another out of the house
- to neglect another when he or she is sick or pregnant
- to endanger another through reckless driving
- to threaten or attempt to drown another

Emotional Abuse
- to say things that shame, embarrass, ridicule or insult another:
  "You're stupid, filthy, lazy, nasty, silly."
  "You're fat, black, and ugly."
  "You can't do anything right."
  "You'll never get a job."
  "You're an unfit mother or child."
  "You don't deserve anything."
  "Who'd want you."
- to do things that are humiliating
- to withhold affection as punishment
- to threaten to hurt another
- to forbid another to work, handle own money, make decisions, see friends
- to force another to sign over property or give personal possessions
- to tell another about affairs
- to accuse another of having affairs
- to undermine another's sense of power or confidence
- to manipulate with lies, contradictions, or promises

Sexual Abuse
• to force another to have sex
• to force another to have sex with or to watch others
• to threaten or hurt another in order to get sex
• committing sadistic sexual acts

Destructive Acts
• to break furniture, flood rooms, ransack, or dump garbage in the house
• to slash tires, break windows, steal or tamper with car
• to kill or injure pets
• to destroy clothing, jewelry, family photos, or other personal items that are important to another.

Types of Abuse Present in African American Families

Sexual Abuse of Children. Most scholars agree that sexual contact between adults and children is unhealthy,[23] whether physical (deep kissing, touching of breasts, genitals, and/or anus for the purpose of gratification), verbal (explicit discussion of sexual behaviors for the purpose of gratification, harassment, propositioning), or visual (use of pornography, exposure, watching others having sex).[24] Often such abuse is a form of incest between a child and a family member, an adult who has some authority in the child's life, or someone the child has been taught to respect.[25] Sometimes physical force is exerted, but often the child is coerced by verbal threats, manipulation, and confusion. Sibling incest is destructive, often expressing a lack of supervision and a sexualized home atmosphere.[26]

Precisely because some of us are vulnerable—as black people, as women, as children—there is a great reluctance to divulge painful and abusive behaviors in families or intimate relationships (and incest probably ranks as one of the most painful). We worry that it will rebound on us as a community and reinforce long-held stereotypes about black people and how they behave.

Rape. Rape is usually defined as sexual contact that involves the use of physical force (beating someone up, holding someone down), the threat of force (such as use of a gun or other weapon), or other form of effective coercion.[27] Thus rape can describe behaviors directed at either children or adults, either male or female. In every case, it involves the lack of meaningful consent by the victim.[28] Recent discussion has focused on date rape and marital rape. Both experts and the public seem to be moving toward acceptance of a definition of rape that includes any use or threat of physical violence, even though there may have been consent to previous behaviors that might have led to consensual sex.[29] Anytime there are factors that prevent full consent, such as use of alcohol or drugs, mental retardation, or other handicap, sexual behaviors can be considered rape.[30]

"Black women's literature is full of the pain of frequent assault," said Audre Lorde, "not only by a racist patriarchy, but also by black men."[31] Melba Wilson reinforces this unfortunate fact by reiterating the reality that this history has made black women particularly vulnerable to the false accusation that to be antisexist is to be antiblack. In her book describing how black women survive incest Wilson says:

> Meanwhile, woman-hating as a recourse of the powerless is sapping strength from black communities and the very lives of black women. Rape has increased in the last ten years, reported and unreported. Rape is sexualized aggression. As Kalamu ya Salaam, a black male writer points out, "As long as male domination exists, rape will exist. Only women revolting and men made conscious of their responsibility to fight racism can collectively stop rape."[32]

Battering of African American Children. Physical abuse of children is the use of physical force (hitting, slapping, use of a weapon) to maintain control over a child and achieve some gratification for the perpetrator.[33] Controversy centers over the difference between abuse and socially approved corporal punishment. Many studies have shown that a majority of the public approves of physical force with children as a part of normal parenting.[34] However, the public often assumes that the amount of force used in most families is appropriate, and hesitates to examine the severe forms of such physical force. Researchers are finding that a significant number of children experience physical violence far beyond what the public would approve if they really knew the specifics of actual situations.

We know that black children suffer disproportionately from virtually every form of stress affecting full and healthy development. Too many black children live in conditions of poverty that deprive them of necessary medical care, adequate food, housing, and clothing. Yet we believe that none of these stress inducers is more threatening to the healthy development of black children and to the stability of their families than intrafamilial child abuse.[35]

Perhaps the most important aspect of basic research that can shed light on racial differences in risk for abuse and neglect is the study of factors creating either special vulnerability or resistance to particular forms of child maltreatment.[36] Perpetrators of family violence act with greater impunity whenever their chosen victims are less valued in the larger society and when protection for them is less likely to be effective. For example, our research tells us that adopted and stepchildren are twice as likely to be sexually abused within families, and children with disabilities are four times as likely as other children to be abused in families. Likewise, African American children are twice as likely as other children to be abused in families. There seems to be a direct correlation between how much certain classes of children are valued and how much they are abused. The more vulnerable a child is, the more likely that child will be a victim of sexual and physical violence. Because child abuse rates are running between 30 and 50 percent, we know that the vulnerability of black children is exceedingly high.

We believe that most black families understand that discipline is one of the most significant variables affecting their lives and that the best-disciplined family members escape the crippling problems of teenage pregnancy, dropping out of school, drug and alcohol addiction, crime, unemployment, and welfare dependency. Discipline can be understood as an antidote to dysfunction within the black family and community. As such we affirm the application of discipline within black families. We also concur with research that correlates child abuse within black families to the problem of an overreliance on high-risk, child-abusing methods intended to achieve the perceived rewards and blessings that the black church and religiously oriented black families have often traditionally associated with biblical injunctions from the book of Proverbs, and elsewhere in Judeo-Christian scripture, about strictly disciplining children. Researcher Ruby Lassiter points to the consequences of child-abusing discipline, which can be incurred by such inappropriate behavior of well-intentioned black family members.

> The strong belief in the effectiveness and clear rewards of discipline, combined with the equally strong belief that a lack of discipline and parental authority can destroy a child, explains readily why blacks equate acts of discipline with acts of parental love and a strong family life. By contrast, a lack of discipline in the home is equated with a weak family life and uncaring parents. It is clear, then, that because acts of discipline are perceived as expressions of parental love and caring, discipline itself is not the problem. The problem is the family's reliance on and lack of awareness of high-risk, child-abusing methods used to achieve perceived rewards and blessings of well disciplined children.[37]

Lassiter goes on to suggest possible causes of child-abusing disciplinary practice among black families. She cites two significant factors: stress due to being black in a hostile and racist society, and the legacy of patterns of harsh, child-endangering discipline that developed during the black family's experiences during slavery.

We think that many black families are not cognizant of the legacy or the history that produced them, but they accept and follow the harsh, child-endangering disciplinary practices transmitted to them by their family of origin or their church teachings. In chapter 8, we will offer pastoral and congregational responses and recommendations for safety and healing as an antidote to the abusive legacy and history cited by Lassiter and others. Our research confirms Lassiter's statement:

> Unless immediate and firm steps are taken to interrupt the patterns of harsh discipline in black families, far too many black children will continue to be at risk. The existing child protective services come into play only after someone recognizes that a child has been abused, but the very nature of the problem—the legacy, the often unrecognized act, the immeasurable consequences to the child and the family—declares that prevention is the most effective way to protect endangered children.[38]

Battering of African American Women: The literature on battered women shows that the experiences of women of color have not been represented adequately. Current literature typically addresses the issue of race and ethnicity in one of three ways: by failing to mention the race of the battered women included in the research; by acknowledging that only European American women are included; or by including some women of other racial and ethnic groups but not in proportion to their numbers in the population.[39]

Because of this lack of data, a number of questions have

emerged concerning the experiences of African American women in battering relationships, though clearly more research is needed to address more completely the factors that are believed to contribute to wife abuse and woman-battering among African Americans. One particularly interesting question is whether African American males truly subscribe to European American standards of masculinity.

Black sociologist Robert Staples has offered research suggesting that the explanation of violence among African American males as a means of attaining masculinity is somewhat limited, but he does not succeed in discounting the idea totally.[40] Staples also suggests that children growing up in African American communities may be exposed to violence at earlier ages than children of other cultures and may come to accept violence as a natural part of their lives. Staples identifies this acceptance of violence as a contributing factor to marital violence. He does not deny, however, that the African American male's inability to maintain a superior male position in the dominant social structure of the United States may also contribute. This state of alienation and disorganization among many black males represents one aspect of the African American experience that has not been considered in mainstream spouse abuse literature. Such consideration is important not only because it represents a potential causal factor that has yet to be sufficiently investigated but also because it may play a part in the African American women's response to being battered.

Womanist ethicist Delores S. Williams contributes salient information to this paucity of data by summarizing the reality of how black women have experienced battering, and how they respond.

> Black women's experiences with violence have ranged far beyond their homes. Historically, African-American women have suffered violence in three domestic contexts.

In contra-distinction to international environments, black women have met with violence in the domestic context of North America. They have also experienced violence while working in the homes of white female and male employers in the United States. And they have suffered violence in their own homes and communities.

In their writings and personal testimonies, black women have revealed the various strategies they used to deal with violence. They have resorted to legal procedures. Some of them have used public rhetoric and polemic to try to motivate other groups in the society to do something about the violence black women experience. Some have used homespun folk remedies to threaten those who attempt to violate them. Some black women have told their stories to each other and therefore shared ways of confronting violence.[41]

Williams contributes further to inquiry in relation to this significant lacuna in the research, and offers a succinct outline of how the overall area of emerging research bears reflection for pastoral care givers in the black community.

The violence African-American women have experienced in their homes at the hands of their male partners raises several questions when one considers the existence, nature, and popularity of the [anti-black] Ariel literature and controversy. Does the black male "control mentality" that incites the violence males inflict upon black women have kinship with the "control mentality" of white people (thought by Ariel to be human) that inflicts violence upon black people (thought by Ariel to be beasts)? Have some black men, in their violation of black women, internalized this Ariel view of humanity and the beast, appropriating humanity for themselves and beasts for black women? Does the African-American community need to turn its attention to the re-definition of black manhood so that black women will be freed from violence in their homes and communities?[42]

Jo-Ellen Asbury and other researchers have highlighted some aspects of the special experiences of African American women in order to provide spouse abuse literature with an Afrocentric perspective. Researcher Maria Roy indicates that alcohol or drug use by each of the partners is a catalyst for violent episodes. Although the impact of substance abuse on family violence among African Americans needs empirical investigation, preliminary evidence suggests that it may be a serious factor. As another contributing factor, Roy lists arguments over children and pregnancy.[43]

On the basis of research that attests to the African American tradition of valuing children, one might believe that this issue would not be important in trying to predict violent episodes among African Americans. When one also considers the additional economic stress they represent, however, children may increase the likelihood of violence among African Americans. From this research, coupled with the experiences that follow in the vignettes and analysis of the next chapters, we will offer some resources and recommendations for pastoral care in the concluding chapters of this book.

Perpetrators of Abuse Within the African American Family, Community, and Church

A perpetrator can be anyone who has the power to abuse another and the protection to avoid accountability. No economic, ethnic, gender, or class group is free from the possibility of abuse. But there are patterns of violence within the African American family, civic community, and even within the black church, which we must courageously face even though they are uncomfortable.

First, the abuse of children is primarily a problem of parents and other adults responsible for the care of children. The family is one of the central institutions for the stability of the black community, and the strengths of the black family have provided the nurture that has helped children to survive the brutality of racism and poverty. Yet we must not hide from the fact that parents and other adults are frequently a danger to children. Hiding under the guise of family privacy and the social responsibility to provide discipline for children, a significant number of parents abuse their power and inflict physical, sexual, and emotional damage on their children. Some research shows that a child is more likely to suffer abuse from a parent or other responsible adult than harm from any other calamity such as accident or illness.[44]

Second, men who are not self-conscious and not self-controlled with respect to their socially constructed power, authority, and their ability to maintain control by virtue of physical force are particularly dangerous to women and children in the family. As much as 90 percent of sexual abuse of children may be perpetrated by men. Since nearly 30 percent of children experience some form of sexual abuse, we are talking about a major problem.[45] The serious injuries of older children are almost all caused by men.[46] It is much more likely that a man will batter his partner as a means of maintaining control than that a woman will control the relationship through physical violence. The right to control another by physical violence has been internalized by many black males. The case of athlete-actor O. J. Simpson is the most well-known and notorious; although the example of the athlete Mike Tyson and his rape of beauty contestant Desiree Washington is also well known and exemplifies of this kind of battering in order to control.

The cavalier or macho conquest sexual style of many black men brings into focus issues of race and gender, with considerably less importance attached to gender, and reinforces the idea of black women as sexual objects. The consequence of this is to make black women invisible—and as they become unseen objects, it is an easy step not to regard them as worthy of being loved, cherished, or respected.[47]

As issues of abuse are faced more squarely by the black church, some cherished myths about the black family will have to be reexamined. The first myth is that parents and responsible adults can always be trusted with children. The second myth is that men can be trusted to use the power of male dominance for benevolent ends. Although there are certainly parents and men who are relatively benevolent, the unqualified and unexamined support of these myths creates significant danger for women and children, especially in family settings.

In this chapter we have discussed the nature of abuse in dialogue with the literature on the black family. We have discovered that this is an important dialogue that needs to be continued. Yet much research needs to be done to discover the real needs of black families and develop strategies for preventing violence that is perpetrated on those who cannot defend themselves.

CHAPTER FOUR

Stories of Abuse

In Alice Walker's novel The Color Purple, *Celie, the black heroine, only begins to recover from her traumatic experiences of incest/rape, domestic violence, and marital rape when she is able to tell her story, to be open and honest. Reading fictional narratives where black female characters break through silences to speak the truth of their lives, to give testimony, has helped individual black women take the risk to openly share painful experiences.... Yet many black readers of Alice Walker's fiction were angered by Celie's story. They sought to "punish" Walker by denouncing the work, suggesting it represented a betrayal of blackness. ...And yet there is no healing in silence. Collective black healing can take place only when we face reality.*[1]

In this chapter, we present the witness of persons who have experienced severe abuse, some reported directly by themselves, some through the caring hearts of pastors and counselors. All of the experiences and writers are African American. All have given their permission to use their "voices" as a way of letting the truth set us free. We believe that the topic of sexual abuse and domestic violence cannot be discussed without supporting narratives that give detail and concretion to the topic. We have spoken earlier about the theme of coming to voice. As the poet Audre Lorde reminds us in "Litany for Survival":

and when we speak we are afraid
our words will not be heard

nor welcomed
but when we are silent
we are still afraid
So it is better to speak
remembering
we were never meant to survive.[2]

Collective unmasking is an important act of resistance to evil—that is, resistance must be rooted in a community of dialogue, empathy, and mutual empowerment.[3] If it remains a mark of our oppression that as members of black families we cannot be dedicated to truth in our lives without putting ourselves at risk, then it is a mark of our resistance, our commitment to liberation, when we claim the right to speak the truth of our reality anyway.

When pastoral strategies and ethical values are debated by church leaders, it is important that the voices of those most directly and deeply affected not become lost. We follow the principle that the experiences of those oppressed in a particular situation have hermeneutical privilege to be heard and to help shape the nature of the debate.[4] Patricia Hill Collins argues for the validity of giving hermeneutical privilege to the concrete experiences of African American women because this group faces

> a complex nexus of relationships [including biological classification, the social constructions of race and gender as categories of analysis, the material conditions accompanying these changing social constructions], and black women's consciousness about these themes.[5]

The intense suffering and resilient hope of black women and other violated members of the black family deserve privilege because they give important clues to analyzing the nature of evil and the resistance that evil requires. We give hermeneutical privilege to African American survivors of family violence because we are exploring the root causes and cures of racial and sexual violence.

We invite you to listen with your heart to the cries of the family members in these stories. Listen for the immediate pain, the long-term consequences, the mirror of family abuse with racism and sexism, and the ambiguous role of the black church. In the following chapters, we will develop a more comprehensive ethical and pastoral care approach to the issues of abuse identified here.

Vignette One

Rachael, a Survivor of Rape in Early Childhood

"As the memory of the night I was sexually abused unfolded during my prayer time, I wondered how God could have allowed a seven-year-old girl to be so shamed, hurt, and humiliated. No wonder I didn't remember this until I was thirty-seven years old. I had been praying for several hours when a memory pushed its way from the recesses of my mind.

"It was a cold wintry day. Mama had left me, my six-year-old brother and a four-year-old sister with Daddy while she was at work at an all-night dry cleaners in Chicago. Daddy hadn't worked in a long time, and most of the time he was drunk, playing with his bass fiddle, or gone to some 'club.' Mama said, 'Floyd, you stay home tonight and keep the kids, cause we can't afford to pay nobody.' After Mama was gone the lights went out. I guess they didn't pay the light bill again. I remember Daddy fussin' and cussin' about this. The house started getting cold, and Daddy started drinking. He put my brother and sister to bed in one room and took me to his room.

"I had fallen asleep when suddenly I was awakened by hands touching my body. It was so dark, and I couldn't tell who was touching me. The smell of alcohol was overwhelming. I became afraid as he pushed open my legs and mounted me. I cried out, 'Stop! Don't do this to me!' Then

I heard him say 'It's your mother's fault. She shouldn't have left me with you kids. Don't you tell your Mama, 'cause she won't believe you.'

"For thirty years, this was a well-kept secret, which I did not remember until I committed my life to the Lord. Then, I began to understand my smoldering anger against men, which was explosive and destructive. This act of evil contaminated my past relationships with people and especially men. My rage has manifested itself in many different areas of my life, such as promiscuity, deception, lack of trust, and an inability to communicate feelings and emotions. The silence that was taught—'children are to be seen and not heard'—was the code I grew up with. Poverty related to unemployment and substance abuse due to racist structures and powers were prevalent in my family's situation. I was victimized by these evils as well as many others. But by keeping silent, I contributed to its power over my life.

"One of the ways in which this situation could have been different is if I had been taught as a child that I was a unique child of God and that no one (including my father) had the right to violate me. Also, I should have been taught that I did not have to be silent and that I could communicate my feelings without fear of retribution from my Daddy, God, or anyone."

Vignette Two

Gwen: a Survivor of Rape in Adolescence

Gwen began her life in South Carolina, thirty-two years ago. She has three brothers and one sister. Gwen was unsure of her natural mother's place of origin, though she thinks it was South Carolina. As for her natural father, Gwen has never been given any accurate information about him. At the age of two, Gwen was sent to live with her maternal grandfather and his second wife, separating her from her natural mother, brothers, and sisters, a separation that has endured throughout her life. She was eventually adopted by her maternal grandfather and step-grandmother.

Gwen vividly remembers spending a significant amount of time in church during her early childhood development. Her grandfather was a deacon in the church and actively served in that position. His wife was an evangelist who believed in raising children in a strictly Christian environment and disallowed recreational activities. At the age of thirteen, for reasons unknown to Gwen, she was sent to live with a maternal uncle and his wife. The family, in this new situation, comprised her uncle, his wife, two cousins, and Gwen herself. The first year was uneventful, and Gwen enjoyed her new family life. However, when she was fourteen, her enjoyment was quickly turned into sadness.

The house was nearly empty. The other family members were out doing some shopping. Gwen and her uncle were the only occupants within the confines of the home. "He began talking to me about the 'facts of life,'" she stated. When asked by her uncle what she knew about sex, she simply stated, "I know you can get pregnant." Her uncle moved on to ask her whether or not she had sex with anyone. Again, she stated very simply that she had not. Gwen remembers feeling very unsafe at this point. "He was getting too personal, and I didn't want to talk anymore." Suddenly, before she could complete her thoughts, her uncle became highly aggressive. "He went gorilla on me," Gwen yells. Using his physical size and strength to overpower her, he began trying to stick his finger into her vagina. "Then," Gwen continues, "he began trying to insert his penis." Even though Gwen screamed and fought her uncle, he was able to successfully penetrate her. He succeeded in the rape of his sister's child. For the next fifteen to twenty minutes, Gwen's uncle continued to violate her body and mind. "Did you continue to scream?" I asked. "Yes, until it was over," she responded. Of course, there was no one at home to hear or respond to her cry for help.

For approximately one year, these sexual acts continued against Gwen. When I asked her why she "seemed" to allow these acts of violence to continue, she stated that her uncle had threatened to send her "back down South." Gwen's uncle and his wife were actively involved with the church (they both sang in the choir). However there were no church activities during the week. Gwen was allowed an incredible amount of recreational time and developed friendships with children her own age. Over the course of the next year, given the opportunity to interact with her peers in a social and playful environment, Gwen withstood the sexual abuse. Gwen recalls simply realizing one day that she was paying an awful "high price" for free time and concluded she would be better off with her adopted mother in the South. Soon after this realization, Gwen did move back down South.

After her first encounter with her uncle, when she was "forced to have sex with him," Gwen had feelings of guilt, "like it was my fault," she stated. Compounding her feelings of guilt were the religious beliefs that were instilled in her. "I felt I didn't deserve God's love," she stated. Moreover, she did not feel she had a right to live. She had many questions, one of which had to do with whether or not she really was a member of this family. Not long after returning to the South Gwen decided the answers to her questions could be easily solved by starting a family of her own. She soon married.

After a very short marriage, Gwen became estranged from her husband. She had given birth to one son and was pregnant with her second child at the time of the separation. As an adult, Gwen now feels that the acts of sexual abuse have had a profound effect on her life. She felt her problematic marriage was the result of her early teenage trauma. This, she stated, was because she was always feeling worthless. "Sometimes I understand that it wasn't my fault. Other times I believe it was." During the periods when she felt it was her fault, Gwen recalled moments of putting herself down. When her marriage did not work out, Gwen believed it to be the result of having been "judged": with the end of the marriage, she had been "punished"!

Vignette Three

Doris: a Survivor of Physical Abuse

Doris lives in a federal housing development, just four doors away from the apartment she lived in as a child. Doris has been familiar with the Department of Children and Family Services (DCFS) since they came to investigate her family's home when she was eleven years old. Her teacher had reported that she was pregnant by her mother's boyfriend. Her mother had beaten her when she found out. Doris told DCFS that she had lied about the boyfriend and that someone else had beaten her. Yet everyone in the family knew that her only lie was to the DCFS.

Last year DCFS met with Doris at school. They wanted her to explain why her kids were out of school so much and why they had whelps and bruises all over their bodies. She was told that she needed to learn "positive disciplining skills" and that she should consider moving out of the projects. DCFS set up a monitoring schedule, but they did not keep in touch. She did like the idea of moving, but she could not read and did not even know how to look for a place. She was particularly afraid of getting on the wrong bus and getting lost in a white neighborhood.

DCFS is back in her life again because she stabbed her pregnant thirteen-year-old daughter all over her face and arms with an ordinary fork. No one knows what precipitated the incident. The girl was in a shelter for a few days, but the judge let her come back home with her mother and seven brothers and sisters. Once again, the DCFS workers suggested that she move out of the projects and once again told her that they would monitor her behavior and report back to the court. Doris says that she is not worried about DCFS. "They don't care nothing about no poor black women on aid living in the projects. They are too scared to even come up here. They don't care about me or my kids, and they sho' 'nuff don't care nothing about no pregnant thirteen-year-old black girl. I won't see them no more." Doris is twenty-four years old.

Vignette Four

Shana: a Story of Failed Intervention

"As a youth minister I had the unique opportunity to develop a youth program and close relationships with about twenty-five young people age ten to sixteen. Through the weekly Friday evening programs, special programs, weekly gospel choir practices, and Sunday services, these young people looked forward to the Sunday liturgy, found their role and place within their Catholic Church Community, discovered their African heritage, and realized their black Christian experience. Slowly they developed toward maturity through spiritual and personal growth experiences. The youth discovered self-worth, self-confidence, and self-esteem. They valued themselves, others, and what they offered to their church.

"One of the significant results of this was the disclosure to me by one of the young girls in the youth group that she was pregnant and had been sexually abused by her stepfather since she was five years old. This posed a serious problem because the stepfather was considered a pillar of the church community and his family was well-respected and held in high regard in our church community.

"Upon her disclosure I immediately consulted the Pastoral Team, and together we considered the best avenue for reporting this information with minimal repercussions to the children in the family. We explored options available to young girls in her position. Shana (to give her a name) decided, with our consultation, that she would make the disclosure to the guidance counselor at her high school. She asked me, as her youth minister, to be present while she revealed what had occurred. After she made her report, the bureaucracy took over immediately. The other children in the family were picked up from school and placed in a foster home.

"Some immediate positive effects were:
- For a while I was allowed to visit the children. (There were four children, three from two previous relationships and one from the present.)
- They were all placed together; then the boy was removed and placed in a separate home.
- I was able to shop with the pregnant teenager because she had no clothes to wear.
- They were able to continue to come to church on Sunday for a while.
- They were able to visit my home.
- They continued to get support with the youth group each week.

"There was an immediate negative impact on me. The identity of the person who reports abuse was supposed to be kept confidential. But my identity was revealed, and I was blamed for spreading lies about this man. Shana was called a liar because she said she had been abused since she was five years old. Her stepfather's sisters approached me after Mass and said that Shana was lying and that what she was saying was impossible. The parents, when attending the court hearing, told the judge that I had encouraged these children to lie on them, that my sister had married his son, and that I was jealous of them.

"Shortly thereafter, my visits with the children had to be supervised. It was during these visits that the social worker told me that there were documents to prove that the girls were examined and that there was evidence of sexual abuse, except for the youngest girl who was his biological daughter. Other disclosures were also made:

- Other children (young girls) in the block had been sexually abused by him.
- The stepfather's ex-wife's sister had been abused by him while living in their home, and no one had said anything.
- The social worker knew about his abuse many years ago because she was a friend of his ex-wife and knew the family well.
- The mother refused to give up the stepfather because she would not go back to a welfare lifestyle.

"After one year, which included counseling, Shana and her sisters were returned home to the mother and stepfather. I was informed that the goal of the Social Services Agency was to keep the family together. Shana had a baby boy and the stepfather and mother worked their way back into the church community. He continued to abuse both girls. Shana came to me to let me know in so many words that "it" continued, but we learned that nothing would change. Shana graduated from high school, got a good job working with construction engineers, and played a significant role in planning a local expressway. She is married now and has another child and seems to be doing all right.

"In dealing with the situation initially, I felt that the right thing was being done and that the children were going to be protected; instead, the church and I had to endure lies that affected our lives. The children were ostracized by members of our community until they stopped coming to church. After this experience, I vowed that I would never again send children through the social service system. As a school principal, I have advised and counseled children on how to protect themselves, how to be proactive. I have worked to empower children and invite agencies to assist them with the tools to provide for their own safety."

Vignette 5

Jeremy: a Male Survivor of Sexual Abuse
"Recalling this experience is one of the most painful activities that I have ever engaged in. My memory of this story was repressed for many years. Now it unfolds like to a rising mist, unveiling the hidden dangers of a jungle. Every time I recall what happened, I remember it with greater clarity and increased animosity. For nearly ten years, until I was nineteen, I had forgotten that I was a victim of sexual violence. I believe it happened when I was in elementary school between the fourth and fifth grades. If it were not for the simultaneous experiences of the death of my grandfather and the rape of my best friend, I am convinced, I would have never recalled this painful memory.

"The context is my childhood neighborhood—low-rise projects. The inhabitants of these projects were black and white, working-poor or AFDC recipients. Across the street from our apartment lived a dingy middle-aged white man. He was divorced and unemployed. He spent most of his time helping the youth of the community repair bicycles, go-carts, cars, and other gadgets. In his yard the grass was worn, displaying the traffic patterns of his visitors as well as their continued meeting space. My brother (two years younger than I) and I were frequent visitors to this hang-out, outside in the yard. We never went inside; as I remember, very few children did. Everyone thought that they would get the "cooties" if they went inside his house—being that he was a dirty old man.

"However, one day this changed. Somehow, my brother and I were inside the house that we vowed never to go in. We were sitting on his dusty sofa, dodging gigantic flies, fanning the smell of undisposed garbage, looking at pornographic comic pictures. I do not recall if I was excited, or if the comics were of a heterosexual or homosexual nature. I only remember giggling and laughing while the old white man and his young black accomplice egged us on to continue laughing. My brother and I knew both of them well. The black accomplice was our neighbor to the east and the white man was our neighbor to the north.

"I do not recall walking into his apartment, much less being invited. Neither do I recall how my brother and I were separated. He was in one bedroom with the black man, and I was in the other with the white guy. He got my pants down and penetrated my anus. Presumably, at the same time, the black guy was doing the same thing to my brother. The two perpetrators arranged their molestation of us in such a way as to see what the other was doing since the rooms were situated kitty-corner to each other. Despite our pleas and cries, our perpetrators looked at each other and encouraged each other not to stop. Even as I heard the perpetrators encouraging each other, I heard my brother's piercing voice, "Stop, it hurts." As my pain grew more and more unbearable, my cries became louder and louder, and I kicked and begged him to stop.

"Just as suddenly as it started, it ended. My brother and I were in our apartment. Once again, I do not know how we got out or how long we stayed with our perpetrators. I only know that we went home and told our parents. I have no recollection of telling my mother or father; I have only their command that we were never to go across the street again or play with either one of our perpetrators. The police arrived. To whom they spoke, I do not know. I am convinced, though, that their arrival and interview was about our molestation. Yet, I do not remember speaking to any officer or counselor about what had taken place.

"Time passed after this ordeal. Our perpetrators moved away, as did we. But our family never discussed the molestation of my brother and me. We talked about everything in our family—sex, rape, racism, responsibility, religion, and so on—but we never talked about this ordeal. Not only has the family unit as a whole failed to help me, my brother and I never talked about it with each other. Were we given instructions to forget the entire matter? Maybe. I cannot remember. Even with the fear of certain and severe retaliation for any wrong-doing of any of my brothers, we always talked to each other. But my brother and I never communicated to each other about this story after it happened, verbally or otherwise."

Vignette 6

Joyce: a Survivor of Battering and Rape
"My parents were dressing for success and going out on the town. Again. I was raised in a black family whose social status was upwardly mobile in both aspirations and realizations, and my folks prided themselves on the social clubs to which they belonged and those events which secured their status as 'glitterati niggarati,' as my mother would say. This time I was about eight; I remember standing in the bathroom as my mother, standing in front of the mirror, smoothed her black hair with its newly applied copper streak in place. As my father passed by, tuxedo in hand on his way to get dressed, she said to him, 'Honey, I'm going to be real black for you!'

"He stopped in his tracks, glancing over the new hairdo.

I could see his rage rising. 'You look like a nigger whore!'
He liked his women light, bright, almost white, as befitting
his status as a successful black male, although one whose
employment and education were much less than that of my
successful, professional mother. Somehow, on this night,
the reddish streak in my mother's hair displeased him, did
not meet his standards. This night he seemed unusually
'ready to rumble.'

"His anger, however, was not unusual in preparing for
an evening out. Usually they began drinking long before
they went anywhere. Alcohol lessened their anxiety about
the pressures that went with trying to make it with the in-
crowd. It lessened his insecurities about how she was the
more accomplished of the two when they were in settings
in which he depended on her to make a way for them to
look good in public. Alcohol and abuse went hand in hand
as constant companions in the horror of domestic and sexual violence that was a regular part of my life for my entire
childhood and adolescence.

"On this occasion, his anger expanded when he noticed
me now crouching near the bathroom door, flinching
already from the tone of his voice. 'I suppose you want
your hair to look this way too, huh?' My parents prided
themselves on my 'good' hair—hair that was like white
folks'—long, straight, and definitely not nappy. In a sud-
den sweep he slapped my mother full in the face. He then
slapped me—just for seeing this happen. In another sud-
den move, he grabbed my mother by the hair and began
beating her, pushing her face into the wash basin, running
water to rinse out what she had put in as a treat just for
him—a hint of 'bad girl' glamour popular at the time.

"She was screaming. Screaming as she always did, curs-
ing him and clawing him, as she always did—resisting his
violence with her own tirade of language that followed
every fight they ever had. He continued beating while he

pulled her toward the bedroom, where he pulled off her party dress and pushed her onto their bed, which was positioned beneath a crucifix on the wall—a reminder of how God watched over and safeguarded us while we slept. He was ready to rape, to brutalize her into silence and submission as his final way of gaining control. I followed, looking for a way I could help her, knowing that it was beyond my control. This scenario had played itself out so many times before. I was screaming too. 'Daddy, she didn't mean it! Daddy, please don't do it! Daddy, I'll take care of her....' Sometimes my own screaming would shame him or stop him in his wrath. This night it did not.

"This night his rage extended to me, as it occasionally did. Furious, frustrated, perhaps frightened by his own anger, he finished with her and reached for me. 'Don't you ever tell....' " he began, as my own body bent to his anger, and bent to his body intruding into mine, intruding until my own screaming stilled to silence.

"The violence was over. Physical violence was over—it was quiet once again in the house. I crept back to my room, telling him and telling my mother that I would be a good girl—a promise I regularly made when violence occurred. I believed that if I were a good girl, somehow I might forestall what regularly went on. I fixed my gaze on the crucifix on my own bedroom wall, silently begging God to make things better.

"I knew that my mother would never submit passively to my father's rage, but I always thought that if she would just not 'push' him to the point that he would become abusive, no one would get hurt. I faulted her for not being a compliant victim; I excused him for being violent. Somehow, I faulted myself for not being able to prevent what happened with regularity, with consistency, with increasing pain for everyone involved.

"My mother had taught me very well how to be a 'good

girl.' She herself taught me how to French kiss, sticking her tongue in my mouth, teaching me the ways that would make me attractive to men like my father. 'This is what our men want,' she would say. My mother also regularly exposed her body to me in the bathroom, showing me how to fondle myself, to pleasure myself, in case I could not find a black man good enough for me.

"The lessons she taught me were right there in my memory as I stood in the bathroom with her that night, watching as she made herself beautiful for the man who regularly abused her, and me for being like her. Made in my parents' image: *beautiful* according to the black physical standards they had set for themselves; *brilliant* and socially acceptable according to the intellectual and social standards they had set for themselves. *Battered and confused* by the mixed messages they consistently broadcast by their own behavior, I became the quintessential model of the phrase so frequently applied to children of my generation—'Young, gifted, and black!'

"Everyone in the social and upwardly mobile black community in which my parents regularly participated knew what went on in my house. This fact was verified for me over and over during conversations with relatives and friends following the deaths of both of my parents. My parents' pastor and the many clergy and religious leaders who also frequented our home all knew of the violence and the vengeance. Not one of them ever intervened.

"Years of struggle to gain a sense of self-esteem, years of psychotherapy to heal a scarred and scary past have allowed me to know that God was with me, providing me with a way to go on and to get free of the past."

CHAPTER FIVE

Pastoral Analysis of Abuse

The stories of Rachael, Gwen, Doris, Shana, Jeremy, and Joyce are troubling because they present such clear injustice and evil in the lives of black families. The children and women had little choice about how they were treated and few resources they could draw on to change their situations. Yet even in the midst of such evil, there are important clues that can provide a starting point for understanding the dynamics of abuse and healing in the context of African American family units.[1]

Resistance to Abuse

One of the most important characteristics in the vignettes in chapter 4 is the resistance of victims to the violence that was done to them. Even the youngest children recognized that they were being mistreated and objected to their abuser about what was happening, even though they could not prevent the consequent harm that was done to their bodies and spirits. Our study of family violence has led us to see active resistance to abuse of power and experiences of violence as a defining characteristic in the lives of black survivors. Resistance to violence has been picked up by womanist scholars as a theme for theology and ethics. For example, Patricia Hill Collins has written about the hidden consciousness of black women who resisted rape and physical abuse during slavery and thus created communities of resistance to white supremacy and its violence.[2] We see this resistance in the stories we have been told by survivors of black family violence, and we have learned to look for resistance whenever we suspect we are dealing with situations of abuse. To clarify, we define resistance this way:

> Resistance to evil is a form of liberated and critical consciousness that enables persons to stand against evil in silence, language, and action.[3]

All of the persons in chapter 4 resisted abuse in the best ways they could find. We believe that identifying the forms of resistance can help pastoral leaders become more sensitive to the existence of family violence itself.

We note that seven-year-old Rachael was disoriented when her father awakened her by touching her body, but she quickly oriented herself toward the abusiveness of what was happening. She says, "The smell of alcohol was overwhelming. I became afraid as he pushed open my legs and mounted me. I cried out, 'Stop! Don't do this to me!'" Her immediate visceral reaction was that what was happening was wrong. She was being raped, and even though she was only a child and could not fully understand what was happening, she knew that she was being treated destructively. Even in situations in which young children are manipulated into collusion with the abuser, there is a strong awareness that something is not right. As a young child, Rachael was not able to protect herself, but she still reacts with revulsion when she remembers the trauma of that defining moment in her life. Even as an adult, she resists accepting the reality of what was done to her by her own father.

In the story of Gwen, we learned that she was fourteen when her uncle raped her. He began talking to her about sex and virginity. "Gwen remembers feeling very unsafe at this point. 'He was getting too personal and I didn't want to talk anymore.' Suddenly, before she could complete her thoughts, her uncle became highly aggressive. 'He went gorilla on me,' Gwen yelled. Using his physical size and strength to overpower her, he began trying to stick his finger into her vagina. 'Then,' Gwen continues, 'he began trying to insert his penis.' Even though Gwen screamed and fought her uncle, he was able to successfully penetrate her." Here we see a clear example of resistance, fighting to protect herself even though her physical struggle may have endangered her more. Her resistance is a sign that evil is present.

In some cases of adolescent abuse, the perpetrator manipulates, coerces, and threatens the victim into compliance. Many victims are so terrorized that they cannot verbally or physically resist. Some adults mistake adolescent compliance as consent, thereby disregarding the tactics of terror available to the adult. Another form of resistance is body numbness. If the child cannot prevent the abuse, she can refuse to accept the reality of the violence done to her. Dissociation is a psychological defense whereby a child departs from her body by concentrating on the ceiling or another object in the room.[4] Many victims who have been molested over a period of time can tell vividly about the physical arrangements of the room, but may not be able to describe the sexual behaviors of the perpetrator. Even children who have been physically abused often have amnesia about what actually happened. Jeremy forgot for ten years that he had been molested by a neighbor. The forgetting is actually a form of resistance, the refusal to cooperate with the experience of being violated. The child may not be able to prevent the violence, but he or she can refuse to identify with the violence as a definition of self. Sometimes silence is a form of resistance to evil, especially if the people in authority are not likely to believe the person who is most vulnerable.

Doris reported to her teacher that she was pregnant from

her mother's boyfriend, but later recanted when threatened by her family. She was more afraid of her family than of DCFS.[5] And when DCFS twice intervened in her life as an adult, her resistance to the terror of her life took the form of anger at the system. "They don't care nothing about no poor black woman on aid living in the projects. They are too scared to even come up here. They don't care about me or my kids, and they sho' 'nuff don't care nothing about no pregnant thirteen-year-old black girl." Implicit in this anger is a wish that someone with authority could do something. Why trust in DCFS when it would not do anything? But would it not be good to find someone who *could* do something, someone who could find decent housing, who could find decent income, who could provide prenatal care for her grandchild, who could protect the other children in the home? Her plaintive cry is based on an accurate social analysis and a vision of how things could be different in the lives of black victims of family abuse and violence. She resists the hypocrisy of a system that promises to help and then does nothing. This loss of hope contributes to acting out her anger on her own children.

Shana's vignette recounts that she grew up in a situation in which her abuse was taken as a matter of course. When she became pregnant, the extended family refused to admit the reality of what was happening. By telling her youth minister, Shana was asserting her will against the control her family tried to exert. Even after the failed intervention, when Shana was again trapped and abused, she managed to tell the youth minister that "it" was happening again. At least one person believed her and gave her a base point of reality around which to organize her life. Her lifeline was that her youth minister knew the truth about her life.

In obedience to the wishes of his family and the community, Jeremy "forgot" about his abuse for over ten years. But a significant loss and sexual violence against one of his best friends brought the memories back with great vividness. He did not forget completely, but he postponed dealing with the trauma until he was strong enough to face it. Now he remembers kicking and screaming while he was abused and hearing his "brother's piercing voice, 'Stop, it hurts.'" Observing someone else who is also abused often helps to orient a survivor to the reality of what happened. This memory of his own resistance and the resistance of his brother helped him preserve his humanity in the midst of violence designed to hurt and destroy his sense of self. As an adult, he is angry at his family for not helping him process the trauma, but he is glad that they called the police and made sure it did not happen again.

Joyce actively resisted when her father battered and raped her mother, even though her behavior put her in great danger. "Sometimes my own screaming would shame him or stop him in his wrath. This night it did not." Often children act in heroic ways when faced with family violence. In this way, children often serve as the conscience of the family in the midst of its violence. But the violence can be overwhelming to a child whose own conscience is still being formed. Joyce is typical of many children in violent black homes in that she felt like she did not do enough. If, in her child's mind, she had been more active, more compliant, earned better grades, been more beautiful, maybe the violence would have stopped. And she sometimes blamed her mother, even though she could not control her violent husband.

In the stories of abuse, the resistance of children and vulnerable adults in black families is a sign of hope. Even when children are told by their families and by society that they should obey and love their parents and other adults, they resist being mistreated and abused. This means that there is some inner moral light in each person that knows when the self is being violated. This the black church calls the image of God.[6] Children can be trusted to know the truth. Children are not complete captives of imagination and lies, as many adults think. Learning to trust children and learning to think and feel as a child does are keys to understanding the dynamics of abuse and healing.

The Social Conditions of Abuse

We saw in chapters 1 and 2 that violence within the family and social violence, such as poverty, racism, and sexism, must be understood as interrelated realities. Research has consistently shown that all indices of family suffering rise with increases in social disruption and oppression.[7] When chronic poverty and discrimination are countered by organized resistance, which creates cohesive communities, the family is stronger and safer. The black family and the black church have a long history of community resistance to the effects of social oppression. Robert Hill's highly respected research on the strengths of black families shows how this resistance has been organized over the centuries.[8]

> The focus on strengths in terms of Black family life-styles began in the late 1960s. Hill cites strong kinship bonds, strong work orientation, adaptability of family roles, high achievement orientation, and strong religious orientation as important strengths of the Black families he studied.[9]

As Hill's research shows, when studied within the context of resistance to racism, sexism, and poverty, the majority of black families prove to be cohesive, adaptable, work and achievement oriented, and religious.

However, in the absence of communities that support effective resistance, social violence too often results in increased family violence. For example, indices of child abuse rise with unemployment and poverty unless the family has support from the larger community. Similarly, problems such as alcoholism, drug abuse, and street violence have their effects on families.[10] In the vignettes frequent references are made to the social conditions that were contributors to the family dysfunction that led to violence.

In the story of Rachael, she refers to the family struggles against poverty and unemployment as factors in her abuse.

> Mama left me, my six-year-old brother and a four-year-old sister with Daddy while she was at work in an all-night cleaners in Chicago. Daddy hadn't worked in a long time, and most of the time he was drunk, playing with his bass fiddle or gone to some "club." Mama said, "Floyd, you stay home tonight and keep the kids, cause we can't afford to pay nobody." After Mama was gone the lights went out. I guess they didn't pay the light bill again. I remember Daddy fussin' and cussin' about this. The house started getting cold and daddy started drinking.

Here in Rachael's memories are the social factors that were stressful factors on the family: father's unemployment, alcoholism, underemployment of the mother working night shift, inability to pay heat and light bills, and lack of money for babysitters. After Rachael was raped, she remembers her father saying, "It's your mother's fault. She shouldn't have left me with you kids." While this rationalization is false, it is true that the father in this family should not have been trusted with the children. The consequences of social oppression for the adults were contributing factors to the father's violence toward his daughter.

Later Rachael reflects: "Poverty related to unemployment and substance abuse due to racist structures and powers were prevalent in my family's situation. I was victimized by these evils as well as many others." Although we cannot reduce family violence to social conditions, it is important to see the interrelationship between them. In a black family with more resources, the choices would have been different. Mother may not have been working an all-night job; father may have found the help and job he needed; they may have had adequate housing with heat and lights; there may have been babysitters or day care for the children. Many things might have been different in ways that would have benefited the children. However, even with these difficult problems, this family could have reduced its violence with adequate support and accountability from the larger community. In many communities, this function has been admirably provided by the black church.

However, we know that improved social conditions do not, in themselves, provide for less violence in black families. For example, in Joyce's vignette, which is the story of a middle-class black family, the violence is not alleviated by economic success and social achievement. The pressures to maintain the respectability of a middle-class lifestyle became a part of the rationalization for the father's abuse of his wife and his daughter. In this case, racism was a real stress inducer in spite of the economic success of the family.

Gwen was sent to live with extended family for reasons unknown to her. Informal adoption and extended family care is one of the adaptations black families have made for survival.[11] When a parent is overwhelmed with the responsibility of parenting, often grandparents or other relatives will pitch in. Many children have been protected through the intervention of extended families. In Gwen's situation, however, when the grandparents could no longer provide for her care, she was sent to an aunt and uncle and she was abused. In this case, the extended family provided protection for many years, but then failed to provide what she needed. Gwen's isolation can be surmised from the fact that she did not tell anyone what happened. Fortunately, after a year of abuse, she had the strength to go back South to live with her mother where she was safer. In the story as we have it, one of the social factors that silenced her and made her vulnerable was her age. The expectations about the trustworthiness of children is determined by the church and the larger society. Many children know not to speak of their abuse because they have been told that "children should be seen and not heard." Other messages about the needs of children for correction and moral guidance supported by physical punishment tell children that it is not safe to speak of the horror of rape. Gwen knew better than to tell anyone what happened, and, as a result, she had to endure the violence the best way she could.

Doris's story also shows the crucial role of economic conditions. She lived "in a federal housing development, just four doors away from the apartment she lived in as a child." DCFS intervened in her family life at least three times in her lifetime to cope with physical and sexual abuse, but not in ways that were effective in providing for the needs of the family. According to her own witness, she would have been open to genuine help. "She did like the idea of moving, but she could not read and did not even know how to look for a place. She was particularly afraid of getting on the wrong bus and getting lost in a white neighborhood."

But she learned over years of disappointment that DCFS does not deliver on its promises. She rejected the agency's help because "They don't care about me or my kids and they sho' 'nuff don't care nothing about no pregnant thirteen-year-old black girl." In these comments, one can see the effects of poverty, racism, and a social system that is not serious about helping black people. The federal housing project failed to provide a safe place for her or her family. The schools failed by their ineffective education and interventions when she was in need. Her life was circumscribed by her awareness that a poor black single parent from the projects has very few choices or resources for changing her situation. She is resigned to seeing the patterns of abuse and deprivation repeated into the third generation because nothing can really be done. Based on firsthand experience, getting the attention of DCFS and the courts offered no possibilities for change.[12]

Shana's story is tragic because there was a chance for a successful intervention in an abusive situation. However, the courts and the social service agencies eventually supported the patriarchal family over the witness of the children. The parents were considered more trustworthy than a child. After a period of disruption, the judge returned the children to the home, where they continued to be sexually abused. The ideology of family privacy that mandates support of the family whenever possible and limits the right of the community to challenge the authority of parents over their children served to endanger the children. Family privacy can be a beneficial principle for families that function well, but the rights of children to safety from violence must also be a principle of public policy.

Jeremy, also, was endangered by a lack of supervision in a dangerous community. Pedophiles are people who live disguised as respectable citizens in every community—as poor people struggling to make it; as school teachers helping children; as volunteers with children's programs; as bankers and lawyers. The most effective programs to protect children from pedophiles involve adequate supervision and ongoing education on how children can protect themselves. Even the best efforts cannot provide complete protection. If a child is abused by a pedophile, it is vitally important that the child get counseling to help him or her understand what happened and to deal with issues of shame and guilt. Jeremy's parents were right to call the police and ensure that the immediate danger was dealt with. But then they should have sought professional help for Jeremy and his brother. In fact, the whole family needed help to talk about what happened and decide how they would deal with it together. The adult conspiracy of silence when children are sexually abused is tremendously harmful.

These vignettes illustrate a major point about black family violence. There is a mirrorlike correspondence between family violence and violent attitudes and behaviors in the larger society. The violence, discrimination, and poverty that is caused by racism and sexism becomes a contributing factor to the mistreatment of vulnerable members of families. They illustrate that resistance to the social conditions that endanger children must be organized by the black church and other community agencies.

Incest and Child Sexual Abuse—Why Does It Happen? Observations from a Womanist Perspective

The sexual oppression that exists in black communities makes the development of a black feminist perspective on incest and child sexual abuse long overdue. This oppression allows the tacit acceptance of incest and sexual abuse in our communities. The situation is one in which the abuse (whether regarded as incest, rape, or domestic violence) is almost regarded as a man's *right* if sexual gratification is not forthcoming from more appropriate avenues. The protection of men who seek sexual gratification from children and other persons who cannot protect themselves needs to be stopped.

The need to address the sexism in black communities is a necessary part of the development of a womanist analysis about incest and sexual abuse—but it is not the only thing that is necessary. Such an analysis must also be concerned with attacking racist stereotypes about black women's and men's sexuality.

The womanist perspective must deal with the sexual

oppression that victimizes women in black communities and also the racism that has been apparent both in wider society and within the women's movement. The failure of black communities, and in particular many black women, to embrace womanist principles has meant that the inequities associated with sexuality continue to place black girls and black women at a disadvantage. The process of undoing the damage caused by the sexual abuse of children is an arduous one. The problem is the male dynamic of power over females; however, it also has to do with the inability or the unwillingness, by some, though not all, to examine the conscious or unconscious sanction for uncontrolled male sexual gratification.

A speech by counselor and women's health activist Pat Agana eloquently frames what this failure to grasp the nettle of gender relations in black communities can mean in the context of child sexual abuse:

> Child sexual abuse is not a new phenomenon. Each and every one of us can relay stories from our childhood about particular individuals in our communities who were said to be strange or it was said that they were the father of their daughter's child. These tales may have been whispered, but we all know of them.[13]

Race, Gender, and Sex Roles

Racism and sexism combine to militate against what should be black women's unassailable right to self-determination and freedom from oppression. Historically, we have been constricted on the one hand by our absolute need to work for the survival of ourselves and our communities in the face of unrelenting racism and hostility. On the other, we are chastised for daring to survive, indeed for the quality of our survival. Angela Davis wrote about our predicament in this way:

Like their men, Black women have worked until they could work no more. Like their men, they have assumed the responsibilities of family providers. The unorthodox feminine qualities of assertiveness and self-reliance—for which Black women have been frequently praised but more often rebuked—are reflections of their labor and their struggles outside the home. But like their white sisters called 'housewives,' they have cooked and cleaned and have nurtured and reared untold numbers of children. But unlike the white housewives, who learned to lean on their husbands for economic security, Black wives and mothers, usually workers as well, have rarely been offered the time and energy to become experts at domesticity. Like their white working-class sisters, who also carry the double burden of working for a living and servicing husbands and children, Black women have needed relief from this oppressive predicament for a long, long time.[14]

Again, myths play their part in threatening black women's survival. Myths about the roles of black women and the alleged damage this does to black males, especially. Michele Wallace succinctly outlines the essence of the myth/roles of black women in the following passage:

Sapphire. Mammy. Tragic mulatto wench. Workhorse, can swing an axe, lift a load, pick cotton with any man. A wonderful housekeeper. Excellent with children. Very clean. Very religious. A terrific mother. A great little singer and dancer and a devoted teacher and social worker. She's always had more opportunities than the black man because she was no threat to the white man so he made it easy for her. But curiously enough, she frequently ends up on welfare. Nevertheless, she is more educated and makes more money than the black man. She is more likely to be employed and more likely to be a professional than the black man. And subsequently she provides the main support for the family. Not beautiful, rather hard looking unless she has white blood, but then very beautiful. The black ones are exotic though, great in bed, tigers. And very fertile. If she is middle class she tends to be uptight about sex, prudish. She is hard on and unsupportive of black men, domineering, castrating. She tends to wear the pants around her house. Very strong. Sorrow rolls right off her brow like so much rain. Tough, unfeminine. Opposed to women's rights movements, considers herself already liberated. Nevertheless, unworldly. Definitely not a dreamer, rigid, inflexible, uncompassionate, lacking in goals any more imaginative than a basket of fried chicken and [good sex].[15]

Equally, however, black men are also constrained by another set of stereotypes. A similar mythological role depiction of the black male could read as follows:

Stud. Over-sexed animal. Strong young buck. Hard worker. Uppity at times but can be whipped back into shape. Not to be trusted around white women. Craves white women, especially if he is middle class. Brutal to black women. Dominated by black women. Downtrodden because of domineering black women. Unemployed and unemployable. Low self-esteem. High mortality rate. Strung out on dope. As likely to die from being shot as from drug overdose. Good looking. Fancies himself a ladies' man. Mr. Preacher Man. Mr. Pimp. Mr. Drug Pusher. Mr. Lawyer, Doctor, Businessman. Can take him out of the ghetto, but can't take the ghetto out of him. Fathers children and leaves them. Weak but proud. Violent. Miseducated. A bit slow on the uptake. Braggadocio. Liar.

These stereotype straitjackets, which black people are also guilty of believing they fit into at times, are largely responsible for the problems that have prevented an honest and empathetic exploration of relations between black women and black men. We are all victimized because these mythical attributes are assigned to and believed by black people and others. Thankfully, signs are increasing that black women and black men are beginning to tackle this huge gulf that seems to have grown up between them.

Referring to Toni Morrison's example of good relationships between black women and black men explored in her book *Beloved,* writer Bell Hooks has noted:

> Morrison evokes a notion of bonding that may be rooted in passion, desire, even romantic love, but the point of connection between black women and men is that space of recognition and understanding, where we know one another so well, our histories, that we can take the bits and pieces, the fragments of who we are, and put them back together, re-member them. It is this joy of intellectual bonding, of working together to create liberatory theory and analysis that black women and men can give one another.[16]

Sexual harassment, violence, and exploitation of women transcends class and race boundaries. Black and white men, regardless of their class position, align with each other on the basis of shared sexism. The consequences of this for black communities are that black men who are victimized by racism in common with black women also collude, as males, to oppress black women. This belies a failure to understand the dynamics of class structures, which seek to undermine the cohesion of black communities. Some black men—and it is our argument that it is mainly these men who sexually abuse black girls and women—fail to make the connection between racism and sexism. They play out their sexist and sexualized aggression with black girls and women as the losers. Black men who commit sexual abuse against children devalue black people as a community and undermine attempts to throw off stereotypes and work towards shared and equitable solutions for all.

The sexism of some black men and the racism of the culturally dominant white society results in a reluctance by some black female survivors of incest and childhood sexual abuse to name their abusers and thereby take control of their lives. If a black woman does take action, and goes to the police, for example, she is likely to be condemned by her own community for betrayal and to have her own sexuality called into question by the wider community, thus reinforcing the stereotypes. If she does not, she is left with maintaining the silence that gives tacit approval to the abuse within the black family and, thus, undervalues her own worth as a participating and *equal* member of the black community.

We view the task of womanists as working toward overcoming this compulsion to blame black women for their own abuse. It is a struggle that must make us question any knee-jerk tendency to treat women as mindless objects or body parts. In the last vignette in chapter 4, Joyce agonizes over her tendency as a child to blame her mother for her father's violence. As a child she had a right to expect her parents to protect her from violence. But as an adult, Joyce needs to understand the vulnerability of her mother because of sexism. Her mother did not "cause" her husband's violence, and there was likely little she could do to stop it without a different analysis of her situation. Fortunately the domestic violence movement is helping battered women to see their situations and their options differently.

Black women should be arguing for a respect that recognizes the mutual right of black women and black men to break free of the confines laid down by others, confines which have conspired to keep us all victims by dividing one from the other. Our argument is for the right of black women to live lives unfettered and on their own terms, with the roles they occupy being roles that they define themselves.

Cultural Differences

Another reason for developing a womanist perspective about sexual abuse and domestic violence concerns the need to look at cultural differences in how sexual abuse is manifested in black communities. This involves an examination of experiences of abuse (what actually happens) and how black people choose to deal with them (for example, there is often a reluctance to go to the authorities). Black people need to understand different life experiences: for example, growing up poor and black in Texas, instead of white and middle class in wherever. The womanist perspective provides an analysis of specific instances: for example, who perpetrates sexual abuse. Research has shown that a significant proportion of black girls are abused by their mothers' male friends.[17] What are the implications of such a fact in black communities?

In "The Long-Term Effects of Incestuous Abuse: A Comparison of Afro-American and White American Victims," Diana Russell and her coauthors observe:

> That the experiences of White victims are assumed to be the norm for all minority victims is evident in the lack of eth-nicity-based child sexual abuse research. But the assumption that data on Whites accurately reflect the experiences of the members of all other groups denies the role of cultural differences in people's lives, denies the fact that racism has an impact, and reflects the White bias of most researchers in this field.[18]

In practice, cultural prejudice has meant that child sexual abuse has come to be regarded, as Marlene Bogle and others have pointed out, as the norm by some within and many outside black communities. In addition, ignorance of or refusal to accept the existence of sexual abuse as an issue in nonwhite communities has had the effect of obstructing or limiting access to treatment for many black children who are abused.

A womanist position regarding child sexual abuse is one of challenging all aggressive and oppressive male behavior on the basis that it violates their rights as women and as black people. There is a line in the film, *The Color Purple*, in which Celie tells Mister, when freeing herself from his oppressive presence, "Whatever you've done to me has already been done to you." Black men (and black women) who view feminism as a "white girl's thing" and who regard the struggle of womanists as secondary and far to the back of the black struggle would do well to remember that it is only when all reach the "Promised Land" as whole, healthy human beings that black people and black families really will be free. The black community, the black family, and the black church cannot uncritically dismiss half of the body politic and expect the repercussions not to rebound on all as people of color.

Womanists must also speak to those outside black communities about their stereotypes of black women and black men. Only by gaining an understanding of the ways in which black people, and black women in particular, are oppressed by existing power structures (which an exploration of feminism affords) can the black community in general and the black church in particular begin to change destinies and take charge of preventing violence in black families.

Whatever the manifestation of the abuse, it is possible to see links between experiences of abuse and the theories of race and gender. This does not diminish the feelings of violation for many survivors, but it does help to frame an understanding of the frequently asked question, Why did it happen to me? If we can begin to answer that question with an analysis of gender oppression, it may help survivors to understand that their victimization has a social context, even though it does not explain why. The complexity of sexual abuse and domestic violence can begin to be understood, and black women and men can move on together to struggle for justice.

Religion

Research over many years has shown that early experiences affect how persons feel about God. Children who have primarily benevolent experiences are more likely to believe that the creator of the universe is kind and loving. Those children who rarely experience any supportive and empathic relationships tend to internalize the view that the world is a dangerous and hostile place. In rituals of baptism and child dedication, black parents are asked to pledge that they will provide the love and resources that their child needs to grow in wisdom and stature and favor with humans and God, so that the resulting adult will come to faith in Jesus Christ. The church believes that love and respect form the proper environment in which to bring up children. It should come as no surprise, therefore, to believe that abusive experiences in childhood can create significant difficulties for faith and belief in God.[19]

Rachael attributes her recovery of memory to her religious life. "As the memory of that night I was sexually abused unfolded during my prayer time, I wondered how God could have allowed a seven-year-old girl to be so shamed, hurt, and humiliated. No wonder I didn't remember this until I was thirty-seven years old. I had been praying for several hours when a memory pushed its way from the recesses of my mind." In this statement we see anger at God for the injustice done, but we also see how Rachael's faith provided the strength and support she needed to recover the memory. A sign that her faith is mature is that she can clearly see what she needed as a child. "One of the ways in which this situation could have been different is if I had been taught as a child that I was a unique child of God and that no one (including my father) had the right to violate me. Also, I should have been taught that I did not have to be silent and that I could communicate my feelings without fear of retribution from my Daddy, God, or anyone."

For Gwen, it was significant that her grandparents, who put her in danger by sending her to live with her uncle, and her uncle who raped her were all active leaders in the church. "Compounding her feelings of guilt were the religious beliefs that were instilled in her. 'I felt I didn't deserve God's love.'" In fact, she was suicidal. Later "when her marriage didn't work out, Gwen believed it to be the result of having been 'judged,' and with the end of the marriage, she had been 'punished.'"

In the beginning, Shana had enough faith in God and her church to go to the youth minister of the Roman Catholic parish and tell about her abuse. In this moment, she showed remarkable trust that someone cared, would listen, and would do something. Her faith must have increased when she was removed from the home, and it encouraged her to attend church and participate in the youth activities. For a brief moment she experienced justice and protection from harm, and her faith in God was bearing fruit. But when the youth minister became a scapegoat, when she was returned to her family and abused again, and when she was prevented from going to church, she must have felt a deep betrayal. She had been encouraged to believe that God loved her and would save her from harm. But she risked sharing one of her deepest secrets with God's representative. She was disbelieved and sent back into harm's way. How would Shana pray to God after such an experience?

Jeremy is not explicit about how his religious faith was affected by the sexual violence he experienced. He does say that his family talked about almost everything, including religion, but never about the abuse. Silence itself can be a form of communication. If someone experiences a severe trauma like rape, but the adults in his life do not connect the trauma to religion, then the child is forced to conclude that the two things are probably not related. The fact that

Jeremy began talking about his experiences as a seminary student indicates that he had important religious questions that were never addressed by his Christian parents or pastoral leaders of the congregation. Yet he sought to find a way of integrating his experiences of violence with his image of a loving and powerful God. The religious quest for meaning and hope does not disappear because the church chooses to be silent.

For Joyce, the crucifix over her parents' bed and over the bed in her own room played a prominent role in her religious faith. Even as a child she saw the irony in seeing the crucifix, "a reminder of how God watched over and safeguarded us while we slept," while she watched her mother being battered and raped. After she was also beaten and raped, she fixed her gaze "on the crucifix on my own bedroom wall, silently begging God to make things better." In these powerful images we see the resilient hope of a vulnerable, eight-year-old child searching for safety from the violence of her own father. Yet we also feel the fear that God will do nothing for her or for her mother. The silence of God in the crucifix was reinforced by the silence of "my parents' pastor and the many clergy and religious leaders who also frequented our home [who] all knew of the violence and the vengeance. Not one of them ever intervened." Joyce struggled for much of her adult life to overcome this silence from God and the church so that she could "know that God was with me, providing me with a way to go on and to get free of the past."

These vignettes show the extent to which abused black children internalize the religious attitudes symbolized in their abuse. What kind of world did God create that vulnerable black women and children are raped and battered without the protest of the black church? How can the church believe the perpetrators of violence and refuse to hear the horrible pain of those who are victims of abuse?

Why did Joyce's pastor and the many religious leaders who visited her home not intervene? Children assume that adults know what they are doing and, therefore, that the violence of the world is the way it is supposed to be. At the same time, children resist this lie by refusing to accept their pain as normal. Abuse leads to confusion about faith and belief. The testimony of black family victims who are also survivors is important as a source of truth about the resilience of God in an evil world.

CHAPTER SIX

Pastoral Interventions with Victims and Survivors of Abuse

You are a beautiful child of God. You don't deserve to be abused.
—Words of a pastor to a victim of family violence

In the black community, pastors and other church leaders are more likely to know about family violence than other professionals, including doctors, teachers, social workers, and counselors.[1] This means that the ability of the pastor to correctly understand and intervene in abusive families is important for the physical, emotional, and spiritual health of the black community. The goal of this chapter is to outline appropriate pastoral care that will provide support for victims of black family violence.

Pastoral Care with Victims and Survivors

Every situation of black family violence is complex and challenging for pastoral intervention. Providing protective space for a person who is being stalked and threatened with death is different from trying to help a child who has known physical or sexual violence his or her whole life. In this section, we cannot cover all the variables and complexities that a pastoral team might encounter in its pastoral care ministries to black families. But we do hope to provide some principles of assessment, referral, and ongoing support that could make the difference between life and death for some people.[2]

One of the obstacles to good pastoral care with black persons experiencing abuse is misdiagnosis. Persons seeking care often present a problem other than abuse: an ill or bad child, a lack of parenting skills, a breakdown of couple communication, the effects of economic or other crises, alcohol and drug abuse, and so forth. Although these and other problems may well be present in black families, we are suggesting that when violence is present, stopping the violence must take precedence over other problems as the primary diagnosis. This involves a shift in the way most religious leaders learned about pastoral care, because family violence has too often been ignored as a presenting problem.

The reasons for making family violence the primary diagnosis are simple: physical and emotional injuries from violence demand urgent intervention, and few other problems can be effectively addressed when violence is present. For victims, fear of harm overrides all other considerations. How does one focus on communication skills if what one says might be the occasion for violence in the future? For perpetrators, the pattern of violence is deeply ingrained and it works. Why would one give up behaviors that are effective in getting what one wants? While other problems will, no doubt, need to be addressed eventually, the presence of violence in a family precludes their ability to focus on anything else.

Safety First

The first principle of pastoral care in African American families experiencing abuse is safety for the victims.[3] This statement is obvious once a diagnosis of family violence has been made. And it fulfills the scriptural mandate of hospitality for the persons most vulnerable in the community: the widows and orphans in the Old Testament, the poor in the New Testament, and by inference, abused children and adults in black communities.[4] Focusing on the safety of the persons most vulnerable is a valid principle of pastoral care, but this principle is often violated when someone raises a complaint against a prominent leader of the black church or the black community. The vignettes in chapter 4 illustrate the tendency of churches to believe the rationalizations of perpetrators when they are in trusted positions of leadership and to dismiss the complaints of victims who have been betrayed.

What does safety mean when the dangerous person is the same person usually considered trustworthy by the black community, that is, a parent, spouse, relative, or other authority figure? It means overriding one's usual respect for lines of authority and asking what must be done to protect the person in jeopardy if the complaint were true.

A complaint about family violence usually comes to the church because the person in danger tells someone—a relative, a Sunday school teacher, a children's choir director, or a member of the pastoral team. For example, in the fourth vignette, the youth pastor was the one to hear the complaints of sexual abuse from the children. A full evaluation of the details of the complaint may be difficult and take some time. However, the response of the adults at the beginning is crucial.

The corollary pastoral principle at the point of the complaint is this: **Believe the story of the victim for the moment. Ask what must be done if the complaint is true.** This principle helps church leaders focus on the safety needs of the victim, the most vulnerable person, and set aside for the moment the needs of those with more resources. If the complaint is not true, there are forms of remedy that can be applied later. All potentially serious complaints must be investigated, regardless of the social status of the perpetrator. In the beginning of pastoral care with black victims of abuse, safety needs must take priority. Otherwise, the damage to the victim continues.

In the vignettes in chapter 4, all the abused persons except Joyce told someone what was happening—a parent, a relative, a pastor, a social worker. The response of these persons was crucial for the safety of the victim and for the restoration of hope for someone whose trust had been violated. If the person in authority dismisses the complaint and defends the perpetrator, the abuse continues and the victim loses faith in her or his own judgment about good and evil. So it is important to believe the story of the victim for the moment. There will be time later to do a more thorough evaluation of the facts. If the first adult to hear the complaint chooses not to hear, the safety of the victim is jeopardized and the integrity of the church is questioned. If the adult in authority does not hear, where does the victim go next? It is not uncommon that the victim will choose not to tell anyone else and will become resigned to living in an abusive situation. Joyce did not tell anyone about the abuse in her home, though she found out as an adult that several relatives and ministers knew about the violence and did nothing to intervene. In her wisdom as a child, she knew that she would not be believed. One battered wife lived for seventeen years with her husband's violence after her pastor refused to believe her story. Our responsibility as religious leaders is to believe the story of the most vulnerable person when he or she complains about abuse so that further steps of evaluation and prevention can be enacted.

After hearing the story and allowing the possibility of its truth, the next step to providing safety is to ask what must be done if the complaint is true? That is, what steps must be taken to ensure the safety of the victim and to begin a process of evaluation and referral? At this point, pastors and other religious leaders in the black community are usually confronted with their lack of skills and resources for providing the needed safety. Church leaders, including pastors, seldom sufficiently own their authority to intervene in the sanctity of the family. Laws and mores in the United States provide strong protection for families to engage in their private lives without interference from neighbors, friends, and institutions, including the government. It is not likely that a pastor would be able to remove a child or other vulnerable person from a family against that family's will, and it would usually not be proper to do so. Therefore, church leaders within the black community need to see themselves as part of a larger community network concerned for the health of children and all citizens in the community.[5]

When a child is in danger because of sexual or physical abuse, a crime has been committed. More than just the church's interests are at stake, and the black church must work in cooperation with legal and social service authorities. At this point, the normal suspicion of the police, legal, and welfare systems comes into play in the black community. This suspicion takes several forms: Will the child receive the protection she or he needs from the police? Will the police create another trauma in the child's life? Will the involvement of the legal system unfairly jeopardize the family and their ability to survive? Will the social service system treat the family with respect so they can deal with their problems? However well founded these suspicions are, religious leaders also need to ask another set of questions: What will happen to the child if the legal and social service systems are not alerted? What help will the family get if they are not forced by law to face their problems? The precarious life and health of a black child in a violent family should force pastoral leaders to figure out how to use the legal and social service systems in ways that protect black children rather than asking the children to bear the brunt of society's racism.[6]

When the health or life of an adult is at risk because of family violence, the laws are often more ambiguous than in the case of child abuse. In some cases, physical or sexual assault within the family is a crime that can be reported. New legislative initiatives in some states now mean that perpetrators of family violence can be arrested and tried without a decision to "press charges" by the victim. When fairly applied, such laws shift the burden of responsibility for confronting the perpetrator from the victim to the larger community, where it belongs. However, many archaic laws continue to be based on the privacy of the family and the rights of adults to "discipline" their children, and in some cases, for husbands to enforce their leadership and their so-called "conjugal rights" on their wives. Until such laws are changed, adult violence in the black family will be treated differently from street violence.

The legal system is usually a necessary but not sufficient resource for dealing with black family violence. Fortunately, other resources are available for pastoral leaders to use. Twenty-four-hour hotlines for the protection of battered women and rape victims are available in many communities. Pastoral leaders can call these numbers for advice on how to handle difficult situations, and victims themselves can be encouraged to call. During these calls, a trained person will listen, provide emotional support, offer alternative courses of action, and identify community resources for crisis intervention. Among other available resources are shelters for battered women. Shelters are safe houses with trained staff and security systems where women and children can go when their lives and health are at risk. In most cases the exact location of the shelter is secret, and in all cases the shelter has a relationship with the police department for emergency help when needed. Pastoral leaders should know the hotline and shelter phone numbers and should invite shelter and other leaders to do workshops on black family violence for the congregation. Successful referral to a shelter by a pastoral leader depends on whether he or she knows the shelter staff and has confidence in its staff and program. Finding a shelter with expertise in intercultural and interclass issues is very important for most black families.[7]

In addition to the legal and social service systems, pastoral leaders need to know something about working with the health system. Often a pastoral leader will first learn about family violence because there is a health crisis. It may be a crisis of physical health that requires immediate attention by a physician or an emergency room staff. Whenever a pastoral leader suspects physical injury, he or she should request a detailed assessment of medical need. Often victims have been terrorized into hiding or minimizing their injuries for fear of further harm. For example, one perpetrator told his victim that if she sought medical help or talked to anyone, he would kill her. It is not unusual for battered women or children to have broken bones or serious internal organ damage and yet be afraid of going to see a doctor. Pastoral leaders must know the available health services in the community and which ones have skill and understanding of family violence issues.[8] Some studies have shown that 25 percent or more of emergency room visits by adult women are caused by family violence.[9]

Some child and adult victims present themselves to pastoral leaders in a mental health crisis. Symptoms such as panic, high anxiety, depression, paranoia, suicidal ideation, or fragmentation of the personality may be linked to family violence.[10] Pastoral leaders must be skilled in recognizing such psychological symptoms and be able to connect them to family violence in the present or the past. There is an unfortunate tradition within the black church of dismissing some symptoms as "all in the head," self-pity, or irresponsibility. Religious resources such as prayer and Bible study can be important for ongoing pastoral care, but they must not be used as the only pastoral response in a severe mental health crisis. Rather, in addition to prayer, pastoral leaders must know how to make effective referrals to emergency rooms, psychiatrists, and community mental health centers. Although these institutions are not always sensitive to the needs of African American families, pastoral leaders must investigate which places are reliable and learn how to get the help that people really need. If there are not any good mental health resources in the community, this could become a long-term project for the black church. We must not deny black people the resources they need for safety and healing. Religion and mental health can be complementary forms of healing for people in black communities.

Sometimes victims of family violence present safety needs that are rooted in self-destructive behaviors in addition to, or years after, violent experiences. Judith Herman, a psychiatrist in Boston, shows how the long-term consequences of family violence affect the personality development of children and adults.[11] Violence, especially when it exists over many years, results in tearing down the personality. Children who grow up in violent homes where they have been beaten and/or sexually assaulted over and over again develop personalities with internalized violence. Many of the self-destructive symptoms in adults are the result of chronic family violence. Herman also suggests that adults who did not experience violence as children can be psychologically damaged if they are trapped in an intimate relationship that includes battering.[12] The results of a malformed or fragmented personality are frightening to see. Drug and alcohol addiction are common forms of self-abuse because these substances numb the psychological pain and create a sense of euphoria that hides the reality of one's suffering. In her vignette, Joyce shows the lethal effects of the combination of alcohol and violence in one black family. Some survivors of violence continue to use alcohol and drugs to numb the painful memories and ongoing dysfunction of past abuse. Abuse of alcohol and drugs are self-destructive behaviors that tear down physical health, destroy one's ability to work, and often lead to encounters with police, hospitals, and unemployment offices. Other forms of self-destructive behaviors include self-mutilation (cutting parts of one's body with knives and razors), suicide attempts, reckless driving, fascination with guns and knives, reckless endangerment of the self in a variety of dangerous activities, or criminal activity. Some of these behaviors have addictive qualities that serve the psychological function of distracting a person from his or her inner pain, providing an illusion of bravado and potency, and denying and dissociating from the inner suffering caused by past violence. Whenever a pastoral leader encounters symptoms that are destructive of self or others, she or he should ask about a history of violence in the family or other relationships.

When pastoral leaders focus on safety first for the victims of violence, all of the above issues need to be taken into account: legal issues, social service resources, physical and mental health, and self-destructive behaviors. How can pastoral leaders intervene in a person's life to enhance safety from further violence? It may mean calling the police or child abuse hotline to report an abused child because criminal abuse has occurred. It may mean calling a hotline or shelter to find immediate safe housing and other services for adults and children. It may mean encouraging the person to seek medical attention for a physical or mental health problem. Finally, it may mean dealing realistically with the danger of self-destructive behaviors that could lead to violence or death. All of these considerations must be in the mind of pastoral leaders when they encounter a situation of black family violence.

A corollary principle follows from the principle of safety

first: **Respect the agency of the victim.** When a pastoral leader learns of a situation of black family violence, it has probably been going on for some time already. Usually the pastoral leader will not hear of a violent incident the very first time it occurs. This means that the victim has already survived other situations of violence. An important principle of crisis counseling is mobilizing the resources of the person seeking help, who has probably survived many things before. It is not enough to identify the emergency needs of the person. Part of pastoral assessment is learning how the person has coped with past crises and how these inner resources can be used in the present crisis.[13] Enacting the principle of supporting the agency of a careseeker prevents pastoral leaders from feeling totally helpless themselves. Even with all the resources of the community—police, hospitals, community mental health centers, shelters, hotlines, counselors—the victim has choices that must be exercised. For example, a pastoral leader may decide that a victim must go to the emergency room of the local hospital, and then may be frustrated and angry when the victim refuses to go. The refusal of the victim to comply with the advice of a pastoral leader causes much confusion for the pastoral leader about the nature of family violence. If the victim refuses the pastoral advice, then one must ask what this means to the victim.

Why would a person refuse to follow the advice of a pastoral leader?

- The perpetrator may have threatened further harm for this course of action, which means that realistic fear is behind the refusal. Pastoral leaders must understand the level of terror and fear that is realistically a part of the lives of victims. From the chair of the helpful professional, such terror might be hard to comprehend. Just think for a moment of how your life would change if someone were actively trying to kill or otherwise harm you. Then translate this feeling into respect for the agency of the victim you are trying to help. Mobilizing the resources of the victim depends on having respect for the resources that the victim brings to her or his situation.

- The person may have already tried a particular resource and was mistreated or ignored. Some battered black women have already been to the emergency room many times, and they know what kind of treatment they will receive there. This means victims often know more than the pastoral leader about the relative value of the available agencies on issues of violence. A black child may have already talked to the school social worker many times and have been patronized and blamed for his or her problems. Victims of black family violence are often treated differently than other patients or clients because of the widespread denial of the problem. The pastoral leader must be flexible in developing the plan of action that is sensitive to the needs and resources of a particular person or family.

- The person may not have the inner resources to do what the pastoral leader wants. Violence and the threat of violence are effective because they disempower and damage the agency of the victim. After years of captivity and violence, the inner spirit of the person may need time for recovery of her or his strength. This does not mean that the person is weak because, in fact, tremendous strength may have been required to survive to this point. The pastoral leader must have respect for the person's own evaluation of his or her readiness for particular actions. What would be possible for someone who has not been a victim of violence may not be right for a victim who is trying to change her or his life circumstances.

In summary, "safety first" is a more complicated pastoral intervention than first appearances suggest. "Safety first" reverses the usual approaches to pastoral care, which emphasize the abilities of the person to take charge of her or his life. In contrast, this principle recognizes the presence of real external and internal dangers which must be addressed. Believing the story of the victim for the moment and asking what must be done if the story is true initiates a form of crisis counseling that emphasizes assessment of the violence and empowering the victim through use of community resources. Respecting the agency of the victim means finding out about the previous experience of the victim in designing and following through on a plan of action.

Mourning, Healing, and Reconnection[14]

For many victims of black family violence, both children and adults, safety is an ongoing issue. Some black families are dangerous, and pastoral leaders need to constantly monitor the relative danger for victims. There is no such thing as absolute safety for survivors of family violence. Rather, the internal and external struggle to live in safety continues for the rest of one's life. Having faith in God means learning to live in a world with only relative safety. But for victims and survivors of family violence, the trust needed for faith in God has been shattered. Learning how to live in a world of relative safety without inner confidence in the trustworthiness of the self and other people is a challenging task. It is important for a pastoral leader to remember the reality of life-shattering terror and fear that is a lifelong struggle for many black people and to keep vigilant for dangers in real families and other intimate relationships. Pastoral leaders should not quickly interpret a survivor's fears as signs of weakness but rather pay attention to real danger.

When relative safety has been established, the second stage of pastoral care begins, what Judith Herman calls a time of remembering, mourning, and reconnection.

Pastoral leaders must continue to support and work in cooperation with other persons and agencies during this stage: with counselors, social workers, therapy groups, educational programs, and so on. One must resist the temptation to see the black church as the total answer to the needs of victims and survivors after the initial crisis has passed. There is wisdom in the communities of survivors and professional caregivers which can complement the religious community for survivors.

After a child has been rescued from violence in a family, there remains much pastoral care to be done. It is not unusual for the child to continue to live with other family members, either extended family, a single parent without the perpetrator, or in some cases, even in the same home with the perpetrator. Depending on what kind of intervention occurred, the perpetrator may be in jail, separated because of a noncontact court order, allowed supervised visitation with the child or children, or closely monitored while living in the home. The most dangerous situation for a child-victim of physical or sexual violence is unmonitored contact with the perpetrator. In such cases, the pastoral leader should attempt to maintain a regular relationship with the child in order to nurture the trust needed to tell again when violence occurs.

Assuming that one result of reporting abuse is a breakup or radical transformation of the black family, loss is one of the issues facing children. All children form strong emotional attachments with caregiving adults in order to have strength to live. Abused children are often forced to rely on the same persons who abuse them. Such attachments are necessarily very strong since they must incorporate the abuse as well as the caregiving. This means that the loss children experience when the family breaks up is actually exaggerated. They have learned to rely on an abusive parent and mistrust other adults who failed to protect them.

One problem of pastoral leaders is misdiagnosis of this loss and a failure to appreciate the importance of the child's attachment-seeking behavior. It is hard for someone outside the black family to understand the strong attachments that hold abusive families together. When the pastoral leader distances from the perpetrator as a way of handling the horror of his or her crimes, it can be hard to accept the fact that the child is still attached to that person. In some cases, the primary attachment is not with the perpetrator but with the nonabusing parent. The pastoral leader may also be angry at this parent for refusing to act on the available information and protect the child. Now that the perpetrator is gone, the pastoral leader may have trouble understanding the attachment of the child for the nonabusing parent. But one must remember that these were the only adults available in the child's life, and attachment to them was the difference between life and death. Children who cannot attach to some caring adult do not survive. Consequently, even if the available adult is less than ideal, the child has little choice but to become dependent on him or her for survival.

The result of loss of attachment figures is mourning— strong emotional reactions such as shock, numbness, dissociation, depression, shame, anger, and guilt. Such feelings in their acute stages can interfere with the normal tasks of childhood such as paying attention in class, doing homework, forming friendships, engaging in free play. It is crucial for the recovery of children from experiences of black family abuse to have safe places to deal with these feelings. The typical peer group will withdraw from children who are so angry that they pick fights and arguments every day. Teachers in school become frustrated with children who are too depressed to understand history or math lessons and never do their homework. Parental caregivers at home often do not understand why children have nightmares, refuse to eat prepared meals, and would rather watch television than play with friends. Experienced counselors who can engage in play therapy with younger children and talk in age-appropriate ways with adolescents are important resources for children who are mourning the loss of family and other things. Church leaders should support counseling for black children after they have suffered the trauma of abuse and loss of important relationships.

Similar principles also apply to black adult survivors. Some adults remember the trauma of childhood abuse during a crisis in their lives, such as divorce, illness, loss of job, death of a parent or child, or other event. The unresolved feelings from the past rise up and demand attention. Other adults are thrust into a process of mourning when they have been battered in marriage or another intimate relationship. In spite of the perspective of an outsider who is often ready for the person to reorganize and get on with their lives, survivors themselves are often caught in a period of mourning that takes precedence over everything else. When one has lost his or her self-image and important relationships, these losses trigger the stages of mourning, which must be attended to. Some survivors, to comply with social pressure, try to ignore or abbreviate the period of mourning.

The wisdom of pastoral care has taught us that **mourning delayed** is **mourning made complicated.** Acute depression, shame, anger and guilt turn into dissociation, low self-esteem, chronic rage, and self-blame, which, when they become life patterns, are difficult to change. Good pastoral care givers can provide safe space and resources for mourning. For most survivors, this mourning requires a moratorium on normal social responsibilities. Survivors in acute grieving may need respite from parenting responsibilities, from regular work, from leadership tasks. Some may need extended retreats or intensive residential treatment to deal with the accumulated and delayed reaction to the traumas caused by violence.

The biblical image of the black church as a sanctuary from violence describes the safe space needed for many children and adult survivors of family violence. In times of war, soldiers could escape death by going to the sanctuary of a church where they were protected from their political enemies. We need to recapture this idea for survivors of family violence. When a person has been physically and emotionally damaged by physical or sexual violence in a family, that person should be able to find safety in the church. After relative safety has been secured, the church should be a safe place to mourn the losses that occurred because of family violence and begin to make a plan for a new life. Pastoral leaders, in cooperation with community resources, can make a big difference in the lives of people with such a theology of sanctuary. Rather than breaking up families, the black church would be leading the way in providing a foundation for sound families in black communities.

Healing and reconnection are closely related to mourning. Healing is a result of good mourning, as a person acknowledges the losses of the past, accepts the reality of a broken present, and begins to hope for a new future. Healing means understanding and accepting the traumas of the past and their consequences. Past trauma from family violence means that the persons who were trusted and loved in the past betrayed and tried to destroy the person. Giving up the attachments and idealizations about these people is one part of mourning. Healing means understanding and accepting one's own helplessness to change things in the past, and giving oneself credit for the forms of resistance, whether they were effective or not. Healing means acknowledging the ways in which the family violence was internalized and became a self-destructive pattern of attitudes and behaviors. Healing means letting go of the idealized illusions one had about life and relationships with others and accepting a realistic future without these illusions. There are many excellent books written by survivors and therapists about these processes of healing.[15] Some persons with much experience estimate that the mourning and healing stages after prolonged or severe family violence require five to seven years of fairly constant work in groups and individual therapy. Understanding the importance and requirements of this process would change the way pastoral leaders see their pastoral care within the context of the black family. In a society that expects instant solutions to complex problems, the church must be a significant and reliable force that provides safe and stable space and time for persons who are healing from family violence. Such a witness would give all of us the time and space we need to be the sometimes fragile and yet resilient children of God that we are.

Reconnection refers to the process of forming a new network of interpersonal and familial relationships that do not include violence.[16] For some black children and adults who have known nothing but violence in their families, this process is a constant discovery of new possibilities that could not even be imagined before. For others who experienced traumatic violence in spite of their best efforts to avoid it (for example, a woman from a nonviolent home who becomes the victim of a batterer in marriage) the process of reconnection means recovering hope in a previous world that has been shattered by threats of injury and death.

One of the biggest losses from family violence is the ability to trust. Babies are born into the world with an ability to trust. They accept whatever love, food, and comfort they receive from their adult caregivers. If the accompanying price of receiving these necessary resources for life is violence, babies and young children adapt in whatever way they must to survive. Babies in violent homes who are not resilient enough to survive violence from their caregivers die. Every child in a violent home who survives deserves respect and care. But the ability to trust is damaged in the process. Even adults who experience violence much later in life go through extreme trauma. No matter how much self-esteem and self-respect one has, the threat of death, injury, or sexual assault undermines one's trust in other people and in the world. Many people who have been victims of various kinds of violence will never be able to recover the sense of God-given trust they had when they entered into the world. Lack of trust because of violence is one of the leading causes of self-destructive and antisocial behavior, as well as general unhappiness, in the world. This means that recovering a sense of trust is one of the most important and most difficult aspects of healing for survivors.[17]

How does a survivor of black family violence learn to trust again? Although there are many techniques for learning to trust, the principle of pastoral care is very simple. **Trust is learned in relationships with people who are trustworthy**. When one's world has been shattered by the betrayal of trust by family members, either parents or intimate partners, trust in people is difficult to establish. Trust is built up again slowly, in small step after small step, by interacting with persons who are trustworthy. Time after time, survivors have reported to us that their trust in people was built up, not just when everything was going well, but when someone they were beginning to trust handled a conflict or difficult incident with empathy and honesty.

Judith Herman summarizes the wisdom of the survivor movements when she says that therapy and support groups are often crucial components of the tasks of reconnection. Some of the most intense and private moments in healing are best done in the safety of one-to-one therapeutic relationships. Some are best done in groups of survivors who can learn from one another and work out their trust issues with others who understand only too well what healing from family violence involves.[18]

What is the role of the black church during the stage of reconnection and recovering trust? This leads us to revise the above principle of pastoral care:

Trust is learned when the black church community is trustworthy. This principle suggests two things: first, that the black church has often not been trustworthy with victims and survivors of family violence; second, that the black church should become a trustworthy community for victims and survivors of family violence.

First, the black church has often not been trustworthy with victims and survivors of family violence. In fact, the church bears some moral responsibility for the widespread prevalence of family violence in our communities. As teachers and pastors of the church, we have heard many horror stories about the inappropriate and damaging things pastoral leaders have said to children and adults who are caught in violent families.[19]

One mistake many pastoral leaders have made is refusing to believe the victim and defending the perpetrator. Pastors have said such things as the following: *Are you sure he really meant to hurt you? What makes you think your child is telling the truth? I know Deacon Jones. He would never do the things you have accused him of.* According to many survivors of family violence, such responses often prevent the truth from coming out. If a victim has been beaten or sexually assaulted by a member of the family, and then the pastor says it could not have happened, where does a victim go? Many survivors have returned to the family and lived in silence for years and decades after such an event. Such a response undermines trust.

Another mistake made by pastoral leaders is to blame

the victim and sympathize with the perpetrator. Pastors have said such things as the following: *What did you do to make him mad? That child has always been seductive. No wonder she got her father into this trouble. What do you think will happen to your mother if this story gets out? Don't you think she has enough trouble already?* The tendency to blame the person who is complaining and feel sorry for the perpetrator undermines the sense of trust. Some survivors report that it is very hurtful when the perpetrator of their violence is still a respected leader in the church years after disclosure while the victim had to leave the church to get the support she needed.[20]

Another mistake some churches have made is rushing to talk about forgiveness and reconciliation for the perpetrator without dealing with issues of truth and justice for the survivor. Even at the point of first disclosure of violence, some pastors have encouraged a victim of family violence to forgive, to pray harder, and to make things right at home. Years after family violence has been known to others, some churches still withhold fellowship from the survivor because she is angry and unforgiving. What is missing is the willingness of the people to empathize with the victim-survivor in her struggle for healing and justice, and to understand the harm that was done. The double tragedy in many black churches is that other survivors are listening to these conversations and choosing to stay in dangerous situations in order to please the members of the church.[21]

These are some of the ways that church leaders are untrustworthy in their relationships with black victims and survivors of family violence. The good news is that our congregations and pastoral leaders can learn to do better. The Christian gospel is not a timid gospel about cheap forgiveness and the reign of the powerful. Rather the gospel is about Jesus' love for the common people who were oppressed by the economic and political structures of his day, about his compassion for their illnesses and struggles with demons, and about his commitment unto death for the sake of justice and love. Family violence is a frightening reality in our lives, but we follow a Leader who had to suffer in his day, and we count as ancestors the slaves who suffered but found comfort in Jesus as Lord and Savior. The gospel has the resources to help us understand and respond with empathy and trustworthiness to the victims and survivors of family violence.

How can the church become a trustworthy community for victims and survivors of family violence? *The church can respond with truth telling about black family violence.* The church has heard the stories of family violence for many decades. Domestic and sexual abuse are not new. It is time to tell the truth about what is happening. Telling the truth is one form of being trustworthy. Truth telling allows the victims of violence to speak up in church and tell their stories. The shame of family violence should not be on the heads of the victims and survivors. The shame should be on the perpetrators and on the silent community, which has known the truth but has protected those who abuse others. The church needs to reverse the power relationships so the most vulnerable can be free to tell the truth about their lives and have their stories believed.

The church can respond with confession about its complicity with family violence. The church has often refused to listen to its children tell about how they are beaten and sexually assaulted. The church has refused to listen to teenagers who are beaten and raped when they participate in the dating rituals in our schools and communities. The church has refused to hear black women who have been beaten by their husbands. The church has refused to listen to older black adults complain about being mistreated by caregivers and relatives when they are too weak to protect themselves. The church bears a share of the guilt for the prevalence of black family violence, and our guilt is relieved by confession and repentance.

The church can educate itself about the issues of black family violence in order to have a context for understanding the stories of victims and survivors. Religious leaders who do not know the facts about family violence make inappropriate pastoral responses to victims and survivors of violence. Parents do not beat children because they are bad. Adults do not molest children because they are seductive. Men do not batter women because they are rebellious. These are myths that protect the perpetrators and blame the victims of violence. Pastoral leaders must educate themselves about the rationalizations perpetrators use to justify their behaviors. This would go a long way toward earning the trust of victims and survivors and making the church into a trustworthy community.

In summary, pastoral interventions with victims and survivors of family violence are complex and challenging. Safety first must be the motto whenever vulnerable people are threatened with violence. This means learning how to do crisis counseling, empowering victims, mobilizing resources, and dealing with the long-term changes in our churches that survivors deserve. **Mourning, healing, and reconnecting** describe the various stages of recovery from the consequences of violence. We have suggested attitudes, knowledge, and skills that pastoral leaders need to respond with compassion and justice to the pastoral care needs of those who suffer family violence. Next we turn to the issues of perpetrators who are members of our churches and our communities.

CHAPTER SEVEN

Pastoral Interventions with Perpetrators of Abuse

Nowhere does the Bible give a man the right to use violence against a woman. Jesus loves her and gave his life for her. For your own salvation, you must deal with yourself as a sinner before God.
    —A pastor confronting an abusing husband

Safety for victims and accountability for perpetrators in the name of the God of love and justice are central principles for pastoral care of black persons who have engaged in violence toward family members and intimate partners. In the above example, a black pastor practices compassionate but firm accountability to a person who has not yet accepted moral responsibility for his own violence.

Pastoral care of perpetrators of black family violence is a challenging task because the principles of pastoral care need to be revised in this aspect of the church's work. For example, normal pastoral care is based on the assumptions that people tell the truth to the best of their ability and that they are willing to go through the discomfort and pain of necessary changes to become better Christians and human beings. In contrast to this model, perpetrators of family violence often mislead others about the true nature of their attitudes and behaviors, minimize the consequences of their violence upon others, and have little motivation for change unless there are serious consequences for their violence. The goal of this chapter is to outline some principles of appropriate pastoral care that will increase the safety of black victims and develop accountability for those who perpetrate black family violence.[1]

Safety of Victims First

Pastoral leaders most often hear about family violence through the victim, through a disclosure of danger or injury. It may come directly from the victim, but it may also come from a friend or relative or other church leader. One of the first cases Rev. Rufus Steward faced as a pastor was when the aunt of a fifteen-year-old adolescent came for help to protect a child against sexual advances from her father. Since the father was a Sunday school teacher and member of the trustee board, Rev. Steward's first reaction was to feel protective of the girl and angrily confront the father so that he would stop. Fortunately, he sought consultation from a mental health professional who suggested another course of action, namely to talk first with the daughter and see what her needs were. The danger of too quickly confronting the abuser would have been hearing the denial by the father and then feeling helpless and confused about what to do next. Engaging in an angry confrontation with the perpetrator without understanding the dynamics of family violence is based on the false assumption that the father will feel guilty and be willing to change to receive the approval of the pastor. Nothing could be further from the truth. Most perpetrators are experts in manipulating or threatening others to accept their point of view, and they are not likely to submit to the pastor's anger. Even if they do seem to go along with the pastor, it may be only to buy more time so they can threaten the victim into changing her story. It is not unheard of for perpetrators of family violence to confess some story, cry and ask for forgiveness, and promise never to do anything again, if the pastor will only keep what happened a secret. Many pastors in black church settings have been manipulated by this con game, only to find out later that the victim is no longer willing to talk with the pastor, who is confronted with the strong possibility that the abuse continues. This situation may occur in the black commu-

nity because the pastor may mistakenly feel a need to protect a black perpetrator from the reality of a racist police system. We have already discussed how the infrastructures of
racism combine with sexism to collude in favor of the perpetrator of violence in the black family and community.
Whenever the pastor meets first with the perpetrator, the
latter's denial or manipulation will usually further endanger the safety needs of the victim.[2]

The previous chapter also discussed in some detail how to
be an advocate for the safety of the victim through cooperation with the legal, medical, and mental health systems in the
community and through ongoing pastoral care during the
stages of mourning, healing, and reconnection. However,
often pastoral leaders also have a moral responsibility to provide pastoral care for the perpetrator. At the point of disclosure, what are these principles of pastoral care?

Accountability

A key word for beginning work with perpetrators of
black family violence is *accountability*.[3] Nearly all professionals working in the field of family violence agree that
perpetrators do not stop their violence until they face consequences severe enough to force them to change. Adults
who batter their intimate partners have learned a pattern of
behavior that gives them control and dominance in this
relationship, and they are not likely to change without sufficient motivation. Adults who sexually assault black adults
or teenagers get power and/or sexual needs met that seem
worth the risk to them. Adults who molest or beat black
children have learned to rely on this behavior out of deep
needs for power and control, and it is not probable that
these patterns will be altered simply because the pastor
requests it of them. Most perpetrators have a public mask
that stands in direct contradiction to the private tyranny

which they impose on others. Pastoral leaders in the black church must not be fooled by this double identity. "We Wear the Mask," a poem by black poet Paul Laurence Dunar, speaks ironically and paradoxically to this point.

We wear the mask that grins and lies,
It hides our cheeks and shades our eyes,—
This debt we pay to human guile;
With torn and bleeding hearts we smile,
And mouth with myriad subtleties.
Why should the world be otherwise,
In counting all our tears and sighs?
Nay, let them only see us, while
   We wear the mask.
We smile, but, O great Christ, our cries
To Thee from tortured souls arise.
We sing, but oh, the clay is vile
Beneath our feet, and long the mile;
But let the world dream otherwise,
   We wear the mask.[4]

Accountability as a principle of pastoral care says that, for the safety of those who are vulnerable, people must face appropriate consequences for their violent behavior. If power were evenly distributed in the world, individuals would be able to enact their own consequences for violence used against them. A black woman confronted with a batterer would be able to defend herself and then ensure that she was protected from this person in the future. A black child endangered by a molester would be able to stop the abuse and never have to face that person again. The stories of Joyce and Gwen would not end in tragic realizations and undeserved suffering expanded through innocent lives. The vignettes in chapter 4 illustrate that family violence always occurs in interpersonal relationships of inequality. Violence is a learned behavior in that perpetrators are skilled at using violence to get what they want and then avoiding the consequences for their behaviors. This learned pattern—that violence works, that is, a person can get what he wants if he can avoid negative consequences—is irresistible for some people. The existence of violence as a learned, effective behavior is what needs to change in order for justice to be done within the setting of the black family. Justice means, among other things, that the use of destructive power is ethically disallowed, and when it occurs, there are immediate consequences, which protect vulnerable persons from further harm. The "Power and Control Wheel" was developed to illustrate the various forms of power and control that are backed up by violence in families.[5]

Accountability in situations of inequality—such as those between adults and children, men and women, big people and small people, persons who use weapons and those who do not—requires the intervention of outside authority to protect the vulnerable. When pastoral leaders decide to intervene in a situation of black family violence, what structures of authority do they have available to protect the vulnerable?

First, for the safety of victims and accountability for the perpetrators, pastoral leaders must be willing to *use the authority of the pastoral office* within the context of the traditional black church. Pastoral leaders have been granted authority from the church, and often from the larger community, to intervene in certain ways. They are empowered to initiate conversations with anyone in the community since the wider black civic community is regularly understood to be the exterior expression of the inner community of faith. Pastoral leaders do not need permission to talk with a member of the church or the community if they have a concern about someone's physical, emotional, or spiritual health. This use of pastoral authority, traditionally a mantle of justice in the black community, means that a pastoral leader can make an appointment with a possible victim of family violence and ask that person directly if she or he is in danger. If, on the basis of such an interview, the pastoral leader is concerned that a member of the church or the community is in danger, he or she has authority to seek additional resources to help that person.

In this sense, a pastoral leader is an assessment and referral agent who makes a diagnosis of a pastoral problem and then seeks to provide solutions to this problem. If the problem is black family violence, then a pastoral leader has traditional authority granted and expected by the black religious and civic community to do what is necessary to respond to this pastoral emergency. If the perpetrator is angry that the pastoral leader took an action without "permission," because the perpetrator is a spouse or parent of the victim, the pastoral leader can answer that he or she has been called by God to evaluate and respond to the spiritual needs of all members of the church or community and is not required to ask "permission" from anyone to follow her or his calling.

In this chapter, we are calling pastors and pastoral leaders to use their authority in traditionally known and historically acceptable ways in situations of black family violence. Rather than protecting the perpetrator from shame or embarrassment, we suggest that pastoral authority should be used to protect those who are most vulnerable to family violence—frequently these are women and children, but too often they are also men and the elderly.

Second, for the safety of victims and accountability for the perpetrators, pastoral leaders in the black community must also be willing to *use the legal authorities in the larger community* who are responsible for protecting people from violence, namely the police, courts, child protection departments, and any other agencies that have a legal right to remove the perpetrator from the victim.[6] The authority to legally deter a perpetrator from harming a victim extends beyond normal pastoral authority. In situations of family violence, this level of emergency obviously exists. The time when a victim seeks help from someone outside the family is often the most dangerous time. Many events of serious violence, including murder, occur when a victim of violence seeks help and thus endangers the freedom or reputation of the perpetrator. The reason is because the basic motive for the use of family violence is power and control, and seeking help is a threat to that power and control. When a victim seeks community resources for protection, many perpetrators escalate their attempts at power and control. The threat or use of violence is very likely. Most perpetrators can be prevented from further violence only by the intervention of authorized persons who know how to deal with such violence.

Within the black community, the police may need to be engaged with appropriate caution when police-community relations are not well established or the department is not organized explicitly to deal with domestic violence in cross-cultural settings. When vulnerable adults or children are in danger of being beaten or molested, we must be willing to provide protection for them as much as we would for ourselves. In some cases, this means calling the police and asking them to intervene for the sake of a child. When adults have been assaulted and threatened, the use of the police is somewhat more complicated depending on the local laws. Pastoral leaders should know exactly what the laws are about battering, marital rape, stalking, and threats against life and health, and we must encourage the passage of laws that protect family members from the same behaviors that are considered crimes between strangers. Just because the threat of violence comes from a father, mother, or other relative does not mean the victim deserves less protection. The laws that protect people against physical and sexual violence must apply equally to all.

Third, for the safety of victims and accountability for the perpetrators, pastoral leaders must be willing to *use the authority of specialized agencies* with expertise in domestic and sexual violence.[7] Shelters for battered women and children, rape crisis centers, and centers for abused children are important resources for the protection of those who are vulnerable.[8] In some situations, current laws do not allow the police or child protection departments to protect the victims of family violence if there is a lack of reliable evidence. But after a careful assessment, a pastoral leader in the black community may be convinced that a person or persons are in imminent danger. In such cases, it is well within the pastoral and prophetic authority of a religious leader to refer or take those persons to a safe place. Shelters for battered women and children are licensed to temporarily hide and provide room and board for persons they determine are in danger. When the shelter directors are wrong, the courts will actively intervene to correct the situation, but in the meantime, persons who fear for their safety are protected. Because the perpetrator may be deterred by not knowing the location of the shelter, or because he or she fears the response of the police, the vulnerable persons in the black family are safe for an interim period, during which basic counseling and support are available and the violence is alleviated—at least for the time being.

Fourth, for the safety of victims and accountability for the perpetrators, pastoral leaders in the black community must be willing to *cooperate with orders of protection and mandated family separations over a long period of time.* One survivor of battering reports that her pastor took her and her children to a shelter for protection. After two weeks the pastor was convinced by the perpetrator that the situation was not as dangerous as he first thought. So he went to the victim and tried to convince her to reunite the family and told her the shelter leaders were "a bunch of feminists" who are intent on destroying marriages and families. Racism and sexism sought to deter the pastor from a prophetic responsibility. Fortunately the victim was strong enough to disagree with her pastor and chose safety for her family. As a result she lost the support of her pastor and the congregation. This was a severe setback in the healing of a victimized woman and her children because the pastoral leadership chose to follow rather than to set an example of courage for and solidarity with the vulnerable.

Family violence is not "cured" after a few counseling sessions and time for the perpetrator to "cool out." Most acts of family violence are part of predictable cycles that include honeymoon periods of "wine and roses" followed by increasing tension and renewed incidents of violence. Pastoral leaders in the black community need to understand this cycle of violence so they are not fooled by the heartrending pleas for remorse and forgiveness. Examples in the lives of black families so well known as Ike and Tina Turner can be compelling reminders of this reality. Perpetrators can be very convincing that their violence was unintentional, that they have learned their lesson, and that they swear never to be violent again. Without understanding black family violence, these dramatic pleas play into the naive hopes of some pastoral leaders for confession, repentance, forgiveness, and reconciliation by the perpetrator. However, the experience of frequent betrayal by these perpetrators eventually demonstrates that remorse is not the same as genuine change. Any perpetrator who has been willing to use violence in the past has many years of painful change ahead before he or she learns other methods for meaningful relationships within black families. Wise pastoral leaders within the black community are not fooled by the manipulation of perpetrators, which is based on only one thing—restoring their power within the black family and regaining control over their victims.

Even if a pastoral leader sincerely hopes for family reconciliation, she or he must realize what is involved in this process. When a black family wants to remain together in spite of the violence, all persons must recommit themselves to a process of self-evaluation and healing that will take at least two and often five to six years of reeducation, counseling, and peer group experience. Because the process of healing and reconciliation is so difficult, many families will not be able to stay together. Separation is often the only safety plan for violent black families. For this reason pastoral leaders must be able to tolerate their disappointment about the outcome and to support the orders of protection and required family separations for the sake of safety, accountability, and/or eventual reconciliation.

Fifth, for the safety of victims and accountability for the perpetrators, pastoral leaders in the black community must be willing to *support treatment programs for perpetrators.*[9] Even after a perpetrator has accepted the absence of his or her victims because they are in shelters or safe in another location, he or she may try to convince the pastor that this was a unique situation and that the danger has now passed. Many perpetrators continue to blame their victims for causing their violence. For example, many parents believe they have a right to "discipline" their children with physical violence for the sake of control. Some mothers defend their behaviors by saying: "He wouldn't listen, and I didn't have any other choice." Some black men believe they have a right to beat their female partners if they are "too rebellious" or do not provide the pampering which they feel they have a right to as oppressed black men in a racist society. They say: "I had to hit her to get her to shut her mouth and do what she was supposed to do." Some black men even believe that they are entitled to sex with a woman if they do certain things for her, even to the point of rape. "After I spent $100 on dinner and went to her apartment, I don't think she had a right to kick me out." All of these myths are based on serious misconceptions about the nature of quality human relationships and what is mistakenly understood to be a black man's privilege in a world where at least in a family setting his penis or his power gives him an ultimate and deserved advantage. Black parents who do not know how to be parents should not enforce their desires on children through violence. They should seek help in addressing their own deficiencies rather than blaming their children. Black men who think that intimate relationships can survive violence need to examine their own ideas about what it means to be a trustworthy partner with someone else. Black men who feel entitled to sex based on violence and manipulation need to examine their attitudes about black male-female relationships and intimacy.

Therefore, even after an emergency has passed and the victims of black family violence are temporarily safe from further harm, pastoral leaders must remember their history and pattern of violence in any ongoing pastoral care. It is not likely that involvement in the church and occasional talks with the pastoral team will be sufficient to change the violent patterns exhibited by perpetrators. The mistaken attitudes about the "rights" of parents, the "rights" of men, and the "rights" of gratification in marriage are often too deeply ingrained to immediately change. Even when a perpetrator puts on a good mask at church, he or she is probably harboring distorted thinking and abusive private fantasies. The only way these levels of false consciousness can be challenged is through reeducation in groups that specialize in working with violent perpetrators. Curricula based on the dynamics of power and control, the viewing of videotapes, role-playing and sociodramas, and regular interpretation of negative attitudes and behaviors can make a difference in the lives and faith of some perpetrators. This intense reeducation, coupled with consistent pastoral presence, can ultimately effect religious conversion and transformation. The principle of accountability means that pastoral leaders are realistic about the personal and religious changes required to overcome violence and therefore actively support involvement in special programs for overcoming violence.

In summary, *safety for victims first* and *accountability for perpetrators* are the two most important principles for pastoral care in situations of violence in black family settings.

Issues in Pastoral Care of Perpetrators

In this section we examine some of the issues of pastoral care that need to be reexamined in response to the needs of victims and perpetrators of black family violence: couple and family counseling, pastoral confidentiality, and alcohol and drug abuse.

Couple and Family Counseling

In recent years, pastoral leaders have been encouraged to engage in conjoint marriage counseling and to work with the whole family whenever possible. The reason for this is to overcome the bias of individualism in white society and recognize that every person lives within a family system. Family systems thinking draws on wisdom like that of African traditions about extended families and adopted relatives that is at the heart of black churches.[10] For many problems, individuals can change only when the whole family changes. These insights from family systems theory have been important modifications of pastoral care for black families in recent decades.

However, *couple and family counseling is not recommended for situations of family violence.*[11] The reasons are compelling. Marriage and family counseling is based on an assumption of open communication, safety, honesty, and a willingness of each person to take responsibility for his or her own behavior. In fact, establishing these values within a family is often the essence of black family counseling. However, in a family in which there is violence between the adults or violence directed against the children or both, these assumptions do not hold. Violence introduces a hidden agenda of power and control. The perpetrator who engages in violence in black family settings does not believe in open communication, safety, honesty, and taking responsibility. In fact, violence is designed to control the behavior and experience of other persons rather than foster a relationship of mutuality and respect, the hallmarks of egalitarian, as well as traditional black, committed relationships. The one who uses violence has made her or his will dominant in the family and threatens to injure anyone who challenges that dominance.

In most cases of pastoral care, the perpetrator's power and control have challenged or disparaged counseling sessions with a pastoral leader. The perpetrator has probably communicated what he or she expects will happen in such a session, or his or her will is clearly known by the rest of the family because of past violent episodes. Thus, the session will already be scripted to minimize or deny the existence of any violence in the black family or couple. This means that the communication from the family to the pastoral leader will likely be distorted in order to deceive the pastoral leader and make her or him think in a direction other than violence. The pastoral leader is witnessing a drama of deception rather than honest and open communication. How to provide appropriate pastoral care within a context of dishonesty and deception is not usually taught in the basic or required pastoral care training of the pastoral leader. Pastoral leaders in the black community who have received outdated seminary preparation, or minimal professional preparation, would do well to seek additional in-service training or continuing education to provide current, effective pastoral care.

If, in a rare case, a victim of battering or abuse does speak out in a family counseling session and tell the pastoral leader about the violence, then the session will almost surely be followed by another incident of violence. That is, any honest and open communication about the violence most often causes the perpetrator to increase his or her violence in order to reassert power and control. In this situation, the pastoral leader has endangered the health and life of the victim by encouraging honest communication without the means of providing protection if the victim does speak out. If a pastoral leader is involved in a marriage or family session and for the first time a family member discloses black family violence, the pastoral leader must immediately figure out how to protect the victim from further harm. This can be a frightening experience for everyone if the perpetrator is present, and one can be assured that the perpetrator will do everything possible to maintain power and control and disrupt the pastoral leader's attempts to ensure safety. Under no circumstances should the pastoral leader dismiss the family with assurances from the perpetrator that everything will be fine. This will be the most dangerous moment for the victim as the perpetrator uses whatever violence he or she feels is necessary to restore power and control. Rather, the pastor needs to think quickly about use of the police, child protection agencies, shelters, or other agencies with the skills and legal authority to stop the perpetrator from further violence in black family settings.

This example shows the danger of couple and family counseling in situations where there is violence present. This means that when the pastoral leader knows beforehand that there is violence in a marriage or a family, he or she should not advise a conjoint session with all family members. One immediate alternative is for the pastoral leader to review chapter 6 and the earlier sections of this chapter for help with emergency intervention. A preventive alternative would be to proactively seek continuing education resources and to maintain "backup" consultation services of a professional trained in issues of family violence who has experience with the black faith community.

Pastoral Confidentiality

Another revision of traditional pastoral care in work with perpetrators is pastoral confidentiality. Does maintaining confidentiality mean that the hands of a pastoral leader are tied if the person disclosing does not want the information shared outside of the counseling setting? What options does a pastoral leader have when he or she has promised confidentiality and later discovers there is a genuine emergency involving violence in the black family?

Black family violence requires some rethinking of the traditional understandings of pastoral confidentiality.[12] Most pastoral leaders have been trained to protect the information we receive as credible religious leaders. We all know of damage that has been done when a pastoral leader shares information about sexual behavior with the deacon board or when inappropriate information has been shared from the pulpit. If a congregation knows that the members of the pastoral team cannot keep a secret, information about the personal and spiritual struggles of the congregants begins to dry up. There are good reasons why a pastoral leader must be able to keep appropriate confidentiality with the personal information from pastoral care conversations. In some situations, keeping such confidences is inconvenient, especially when the gossip mills based on incorrect information get started. It is tempting to want to correct what the congregation knows, even when the person involved does not want the truth to be shared. These are examples of the normal dilemmas connected with pastoral confidentiality.

However, it is our position in this book that black family violence requires a paradoxical revision of traditional understandings of confidentiality. We believe that pastoral leaders must announce these changes in a clear and direct way at the start of every counseling relationship so that the guidelines are stated from the beginning.

In our pastoral practice, we often say something like this:

I am willing to keep anything you tell me in confidence, which means I will share it with no one else, with two exceptions. First, if I feel that I need professional consulta-

tion in order to be helpful to you. In that case, I will tell you
I am consulting. Second, if I feel that the health or safety of
any person, including you, is at risk. In that case, I reserve
the right to report that a child is in danger or to seek outside
help for a person whose life and health may be in danger.
With those two exceptions, I promise that anything you say
to me will remain confidential.

For most people who come for pastoral care, such a statement is sufficient to enable them to continue without
undue fear about their life becoming available for the
voyeuristic eyes of others. For some people, the caveat
about seeking consultation is actually comforting because
it reminds them that this pastoral leader takes his or her
work seriously and will seek help from another professional if necessary. Although expectations are high in the black
faith community about the biblical competence of the pastor, most parishioners know that the pastoral leader is not
a trained, professional counselor, and they feel comfortable
knowing that the pastor is willing to live within certain
limits. For victims of violence, the caveat about notifying
the proper authorities if there is family violence is also
comforting, and can often make it easier for the person to
openly share his or her fears. It means that the pastoral
leader is not naive about black family violence, that he or
she knows that it can happen even in the most respectable-
looking families, and that he or she knows what to do
when the topic of violence is disclosed. For perpetrators of
violence, the limitation on keeping secrets serves as a
warning. They can choose not to tell about the violence
they are forcing on others and thus protect themselves. But
if they decide to tell part of the truth, the pastoral leader of
the black faith community is not going to collude with
them by minimizing and denying the reality. Limiting confidentiality on issues of black family violence means that
violence will be taken seriously and that the pastoral leader

will do whatever is necessary to protect victims and hold perpetrators accountable. For a few perpetrators who genuinely want help, this could be the best news they have heard for a long time. However, for pastoral care with perpetrators, the above statement on confidentiality protects the pastoral leader by setting honest limits and providing a rationale for involving the authorities later when necessary.

Although we recommend the above revision in the usual understanding of confidentiality, we understand that some pastors will get caught in the complications and ambiguities of this issue. For example, a pastor may promise confidentiality only to discover later that a child or an adult is in danger from family violence. Some pastors will feel confused about which obligation to follow—whether to protect the promise of confidentiality or to protect a victim from further violence. In such cases, we suggest that the principle of protection of the vulnerable from further harm, which is often the difference of life and death, takes priority. While a pastor may be uncomfortable for a time, we believe it is better to live with the uncertainty of the meaning of confidentiality than to live with the guilt of contributing to ongoing black family violence. Knowing that a child or an adult is a victim of domestic and/or sexual violence and feeling helpless to do anything about it is a very uncomfortable place for a pastoral leader to be. We encourage adult education sessions and discussion of the meaning of pastoral confidentiality. Until a new consensus emerges, we suggest that family violence must be treated as an important exception to the general rule of keeping the secrets of parishioners who come for help.

Alcohol and Drug Abuse

A third issue that often becomes confused with family violence is the presence of alcohol and drug abuse. There is obviously some relationship between alcohol and drug abuse and family violence. Addictions are frequently ways that survivors of violence numb themselves to the painful memories and dysfunction that are consequences of violence. We know that changing the pattern of family violence is more difficult when the perpetrator is an active alcohol and drug abuser. Alcohol and drugs cause distorted thinking and feeling that make it more difficult to learn nonviolent forms of behavior. In addition to these realities, we know that persons in recovery from alcohol and drug addictions do not necessarily stop their violence against family members. Violent behavior still works for a perpetrator who feels justified in getting what he or she wants with the threat and use of harm. We know that significant numbers of persons without histories of addiction to alcohol and drugs are violent toward family members. Violence can become its own addictive behavior pattern. So, given these realities, it is best to think of family violence and alcohol and drug abuse as overlapping but distinct problems which must both be treated in order to change either of them.[13]

One popular confusion is the tendency of perpetrators to blame their use of violence on their addiction to alcohol or drugs. Some perpetrators say: "I am never violent when I am not drinking, so I don't really have a problem with violence." Other perpetrators say: "I don't even remember what happened. I guess I blacked out. I will go for alcohol and drug counseling, but I don't really need to be in a group for batterers." These are rationalizations that take the focus off of the violence and put it on the addiction. In many locations, there is less stigma attached to alcohol and drug abuse than to child abuse and battering. It is more acceptable to some people to be a substance abuser than to be a child molester or abuser. In fact, family violence and alcohol and drug abuse are both serious problems that need to be addressed for real change in life to occur.

It is important for pastoral leaders to be very clear on the issue of substance abuse and family violence. Perpetrators of family violence are dangerous people. Although some perpetrators do not use alcohol and drugs, nonetheless they need treatment for their attitudes and behaviors that endanger vulnerable people. Some perpetrators also abuse alcohol and drugs, and if they want to change, they must address both sets of issues in their lives. Pastoral leaders must reject the idea that treatment for alcohol and drug addiction will automatically change violent behavior. The clinical evidence proves that this is not true. Recovering addicts are just as likely as anyone else to be violent.

One difficult problem arises when a pastoral leader must decide which treatment takes priority. Is it better to treat the alcohol and drug addiction first, and later treat the use of violence against others, or vice versa? At this point in history, the health profession knows much more about the treatment of alcohol and drug addictions than about treatment of violent perpetrators. This means that there are many more treatment options for addictions to alcohol and drugs than use of violence. So the temptation is to refer addicted perpetrators to addiction treatment. The danger with this option is that it often ignores the principle we are emphasizing: Safety for victims first. We recommend that referral for alcohol and drug treatment should be made *after safety issues have been addressed*. This means that the safety of victims must take precedence over the referral of the perpetrator for any kind of treatment. The victims should be in a shelter, in a safe home, separated from the perpetrator enforced by an order of protection, and their needs should hold a pastoral priority for care. After disclosure of family violence, victims have many needs, as we previously discussed in chapter 6. These needs must be addressed first before addressing the needs of the perpetrator.

After the safety of the victims has been ensured, then the treatment options of the perpetrators can be considered. When the perpetrator has no access to the victims and is prevented from causing further harm or threatening behaviors, the needs of the perpetrator can be assessed and referrals made. In terms of the relationship between violence and alcohol and drug abuse, under no circumstances should a pastoral leader agree to allow the perpetrator in the same home as a victim just because the perpetrator is in treatment for his or her addictions. Treatment for alcohol and drug abuse does not ensure that a perpetrator will refrain from violent and threatening behavior. On the contrary, we know from clinical and pastoral experience that a perpetrator in recovery from alcohol and drug addictions is frequently very dangerous, and may increase her or his violence to compensate for the loss of the usual highs he or she is dependent upon.

In summary, we have discussed three issues that are important for the pastoral care of families experiencing abuse: couple and family counseling, confidentiality, and alcohol and drug abuse. The bibliography at the end of the book suggests resources that discuss other important issues worthy of consideration.

CHAPTER EIGHT

Congregational Responses for Safety and Healing

The act of incest alone is enough to cause one psychological trauma and life-long emotional damage, but when coupled with heavy theological ramifications, one is in double-trouble! My father was the assistant pastor of the small family-type, Pentecostal church I was raised in and where God's love was constantly preached; respect for parents was another favorite topic. But the most popular theme was the sinner and the sinner's abode in hell. Well, I had problems. I could not love this man who came into my bedroom and did unmentionable things to me; I could not believe that God could love me and yet allow this to continue. I surely had no respect for my father as a parent. Therefore, I was a sinner, right?[1]

In the previous several chapters we emphasized crisis and ongoing pastoral care for African American families experiencing abuse. In this chapter we turn our attention to corporate pastoral care, education, and prevention strategies at the congregational level. We believe that revisions in traditional pastoral care required when pastoral leaders respond to family abuse also lead to revision of other aspects of the congregation's ministries.[2]

In his ground-breaking work, *Pastoral Care in the Black Church*, Edward P. Wimberly indicates that this is a major difference between the kind of pastoral care offered by mainline white denominations and that offered by the black church:

To learn the methods and skills of the one-to-one healing model requires economic resources and extensive clinical and educational opportunities to which many black pastors did not have access until recently. . . . The black church had to rely upon a tradition of sustaining and guiding fashioned in response to oppression. . . . The black pastor needed an orientation that would help him or her utilize the resources within the black church in the care of souls. The creativity of many black pastors has been evidenced in their finding corporate and communal means to meet the needs of persons when theoretical models were inadequate.[3]

Following in the mode of pastoral care established by the black church, which uses the expertise and energy of the entire caring congregation in the expression of its saving work, we offer resources that require the gifts and talents of many members of the congregation to counter the devastating effects of sexual and domestic violence. Because we affirm and share in the definition of black pastoral care outlined by Edward Wimberly and others as "bringing to bear upon persons and families in crisis the total caring resources of the church," we shall explore the prominent role of the total ministry of the black church.[4] Our principal inquiry in this chapter is: How would the ministries of the church change if the needs and insights of victims and survivors of family violence were given priority by the *total caring resources* of the black church?

Imagine an African American congregation of victims and survivors of family violence. Some members of the congregation are children caught in a web of violence that includes physical beatings, sexual assault, and emotional battering directed at destroying their fragile identity. Some members of the congregation are adults who are being battered and raped by intimate partners who explain that they deserve to be treated this way. Some members of the congregation are adults who feel the post-traumatic stress of past violence from child abuse, adolescent date rape, or adult rape and battering. They have escaped the immediate danger and have created a new life, but they still remember some incidents as if they happened yesterday. Others are courageous survivors who have overcome the trauma of their lives and now serve as examples to others of hope and courage in the midst of great adversity.

This description is not far from the truth in many African American congregations. We know that many members of every congregation are caught in violent families or are recovering from the effects of past violence. Some research suggests that in any congregation the percentage of victims and survivors of family violence may be 50 percent or higher. And if we assume that many people come to the black church for healing and safety because of the promises of the gospel, then the percentage could be even higher in many congregations. Just as we assume that the members of our congregations know the devastating effects of the many forms of white racism, so we should assume that half or more of our members have experienced violence within black families because perpetrators take advantage of age, gender, sexual orientation, disabling condition, or other vulnerabilities.

How should the total caring resources and ministries of the black church be organized to respond to the needs and utilize the wisdom of victims and survivors of family violence? Fortunately, we have heard many stories about how congregations are responding creatively and courageously to the needs of victims and survivors of family violence. Many denominations have helped to fund the Center for the Prevention of Sexual and Domestic Violence,[5] which has created much useful material for congregational use in the twenty years since it was founded. The Center has established the Black Church and Domestic Violence Project specifically in order to develop particular ministries that can creatively assist African American victims of domestic and sexual violence, survivors, their families, and their faith communities who want to make a difference in this arena of justice.

Many national denominational offices have produced curricula and educational materials for congregations to combat domestic and sexual violence in families.[6] Unfortunately, many of our African American congregations have a long way to go to respond adequately to this crisis. Dr. Robert Michael Franklin, president of the Interdenominational Theological Center in Atlanta has done much to bring both the need and the means of making a difference in this area to the attention of the black church. In speaking to a National Conference on Black Philanthropy, along with hope for the future he offered a challenge to the present reality of the black church:

> I wish that I could tell you that the awareness around specialized social ministry has progressed to the point that historic Black churches are actively seeking collaboration and partnerships with any and all who offer unrestricted resources to further the common good. The God's honest truth is that more often than we care to admit, without any historical basis for trusting that access to goods and services is fairly allocated, community skepticism results in boundaries which inhibit cross cultural conversation regarding empowerment initiatives. This inhibiting skepticism is often at the expense of women and children who are suffering from family violence. Consequently, many African American families who find themselves in crisis due to domestic violence are forced to choose between secular resources offered by women's rights organizations and the spiritual resources of the historic Black Church.[7]

The shame of the church is that it has taken so long to bring into its public life the needs and insights of victims and survivors of family violence. The church has been silent too long, and we have much for which amends must be made.[8]

In this chapter, we briefly discuss eight areas of the church's life where sensitivity to the needs and wisdom of African American victims and survivors of family violence will make a difference. Much more could be said on this subject, but we recommend additional resources for further study for congregational leaders who want to do more.

1. Use of the Bible in Preaching, Teaching, and Worship

There are two questions to ask about the use of the Bible in developing preaching, teaching, and worship practices that provide pastoral care to victims, survivors, and proactive members of congregations who desire to be transformative in this area of pastoral need. How do the texts, interpretations, prayers, and hymns frequently used in worship sound to the ears of victims and survivors of family violence? What additional texts, interpretations, prayers, and hymns would speak more directly to the needs of victims and survivors of family violence?[9]

Some of the language frequently used in church sounds harsh rather than empowering to persons who are or have been caught in the web of family violence. Evelyn C. White records an experience, which we have heard from victims and survivors many times. She observes:

Yet religious beliefs or fear of rejection from the church may be keeping you in an oppressive, abusive relationship. "When he started beating me I went to the elders of the church. They said I couldn't leave because it would be a bad reflection on other church members. I didn't want to bring shame on the rest of the congregation. The church and my faith are very important to me." If you go to your pastor for help about the violence in your life, you may be told, as the black woman quoted above was, to essentially "love, honor, and obey" the man who is abusing you. Your pastor may read scriptures to you that perpetuate male dominance over women. This is not necessarily surprising since the church (black or white) is a male-dominated institution. It is time, however, to begin to challenge those members of the black clergy who are contributing to the continued abuse of black women through their lack of knowledge about domestic violence and/or sexist attitudes.[10]

As pastoral care givers, we are aware that doctrines of forgiveness and reconciliation can, at times, put pressure on the victim to forgive and forget before he or she is even safe enough to evaluate the situation. When a victim is still under the control and power of the perpetrator, forgiveness is hardly the act of grace that was taught by Jesus Christ. Jesus' parables about forgiveness were told from the perspective of the king, the landlord, and the almighty God. Nowhere does Jesus ask the oppressed or the victims to forgo their claims for justice and forgive the oppressors without justice. Likewise, the time of violence is not the right time for reconciliation.

Linda Hollies, an African American United Methodist pastor who has written extensively on sexual abuse, shares her experience of how a false sense of the doctrine of forgiveness caused her to miss out on the pastoral care she so desperately needed to heal from her own experiences of sexual violence as a child. She reflects on her desire to forgive and to be forgiven after she had joined a new church:

> This God loved me, just as I was; this God invited me to come and receive abundant life. This was appealing to me as a survivor—I wanted to know what "authentic" living was all about. But the mountain [of guilt and sorrow] was still there, and I was not able to talk to anyone. I still hated my father; I went to talk with him and apologized for hating him all those years. He did not understand my pain nor my anger. Forgiveness was supposed to follow my repentance, but I never felt forgiven, for I honestly could not forgive him! More importantly I could not forget! But this

—— 159 ——

newfound relationship with God and a new community were too delightful to turn my back on. Once again, I felt that if I could just pray correctly and ignore this mountain, it would go away.[11]

We are aware that if a pastor asks a child to forgive his father for abuse and to seek reconciliation, a child who has experienced violence will comply in order to avoid further violence. But reconciliation under threat of violence is not the reconciliation Jesus preached. In our sermons and prayers, we need to be careful not to add an extra burden to those who are already victimized by family violence by asking them to be forgiving and reconciling with the perpetrators. Linda Hollies continues to instruct by her own childhood experience in this regard:

> Finally the burden of carrying this secret became too much, so I went to the pastor "to confess." With much emotion, I told my story and he listened attentively, after which he asked me to "agree with him in prayer." When I left, I had two secrets: one from my childhood, and the newly found secret that my "new" relationship with God did not perform the miracle of wiping my memory clean or restoring love for my father within my heart. The fault/blame had to be mine; this was the only logical conclusion. The mountain was yet in control.[12]

Even after years of safety and healing, many survivors are not yet ready to forgive and reconcile. In addition, few perpetrators are contrite and repentant as Jesus requires. When we listen to our sermons and prayers from the perspective of a child in a violent family, the words and phrases sometimes sound quite different and not liberating as they ought to be.[13]

Another example of how victims and survivors hear certain texts and interpretations differently is when we emphasize the sanctity of family and the sin of divorce.

There are biblical texts about the family staying together through adversity and the pain of divorce, and there are times when our pastoral care should emphasize these texts. Family life is not easy, and sometimes adults need to be encouraged to do the hard work that good family life requires.

When a family is a crucible of terror because of violence, the idea of family is not so beautiful, and divorce is much better than being battered again. As we discussed earlier, children are often very attached to their parents, even when there is violence. But this does not mean that it is preferable to keep the family together for the sake of the children. The children need a nurturing family, and they need safety from violence. If adults cannot be nonviolent with their children, they should get help to become the kind of parents their children need. Jesus did allow divorce for "hardness of heart" (Mark 10:2-9). What greater hardness of heart could there be than physical, sexual, and emotional violence against a child or intimate partner?

Another set of Scriptures that can be dangerous in violent families includes the texts about the subordination of women and children to men and fathers. Evelyn C. White reports as an example what we regularly hear from black women who have sought pastoral care from the black church as healing for their situation.

And so, you may be told to accept and forgive the sins of your abusive partner as Christ did for us when he died upon the cross. You [sic] pastor may tell you to read Ephesians 5:21, "Wives, submit yourselves unto your own husbands," and urge you to make the sacrifice for your family. You may be told that your abuse is punishment for being spiritually deficient and that if you pray more it will go away. As one abused black woman reported, your pastor might even say, "Jesus dropped the charges, so why can't you?" ... It is not and never has been God's will that

—— 161 ——

you bow down blindly and accept your partner's abusive behavior. Men who resort to brute force and domination in their relationships deserve strong disapproval and a resounding message that their behavior is wrong from all members of society, including the clergy.[14]

Honoring one's father and mother is a good thing if your parents are trying hard to be faithful Christians and love their children as God loves the church. Parents should honor their children by treating them with respect and love. Some survivors suggest that honoring children should also be one of the Ten Commandments. But when parents are physically and sexually abusive, honoring parents is a difficult concept to live out. Most children interpret honor to mean obeying without question even when the demands are unjust and the punishments are life-threatening. No wonder many children are silent about the abuse they suffer at home. They are trying hard to honor their parents and please the other adults at church. We should interpret honor to mean that reporting violence at home is a sign of respect. Telling a pastor or teacher or social worker about family violence is not dishonor of one's parents. Telling the truth to trusted community leaders is a way children can help their parents to do their duty. Black children need to be empowered to speak out about the suffering in their lives so that parents can get help and be rescued from the sin of violence.[15]

The Scripture about women being subordinate and obedient to their husbands is sometimes interpreted to mean that the man has a responsibility of benevolent leadership in the family, which the woman should respect. However, this Scripture is abused so often that it deserves to be reexamined by African American preachers and theologians.[16] Male headship can be used to force a woman to submit to her husband when he uses or threatens to use violence to enforce his power and control in the marriage or partnership. If we do not mean this, then why do so many preach-ers preach headship without mentioning violence? Battered women almost universally report that men use the Scripture about male headship to justify their battering.

Perpetrators appeal to biblical stories that Adam was cre-ated first, that Eve brought sin into the world, that Paul taught that men should be the head of the family as Christ is the head of the church. Where did perpetrators get these ideas? They came from church. If an idea has been used for centuries to justify male violence against women and chil-dren, then we must assume that many believe this is what the idea means. Many male batterers are most faithful prac-titioners of the idea that God made man the head of the family. If this is what male headship means, then perhaps it is time to reexamine the concept of male headship as the sexist idea it is. We have plenty of evidence that men who believe in male headship are frequently domineering and violent to women and children. It is time we abandon the idea of male headship and emphasize the Scriptures about equality and partnership between men and women and the empowering function of the family for children.

Interpretations of texts about obedience and servant-hood can sound strange when we listen from the perspec-tive of victims and survivors of family violence. Does the Scripture really teach Christians to be obedient in all cir-cumstances and to behave as servants in every social situa-tion? Jesus himself did not behave this way. He reserved obedience to describe his relationship with God, and he used the image of servant to describe how the disciples should handle their competitive power relationships. But when Jesus was faced with the hypocrisy of the religious leaders of his day who exploited the people in the court-yard of the temple, who made secret deals with the oppres-sor at the expense of the poor and who required sacrifices of the people that they would not impose on themselves,

Jesus was rebellious and critical in appropriate ways as the liberating Son of God.

Jesus taught the people how to understand the economic, political, and religious exploitation they were forced to live under, and he was executed because the leaders were afraid his teaching would lead to revolt against the government. Jesus did not teach the poor to be obedient and become servants to the oppressors, but reserved these terms to describe the proper attitudes within God's beloved community. Obedience to God can mean rebellion against structures of injustice. Servanthood to God can mean resistance to systemic violence.

Because we must assume that our congregations have within them African American victims and survivors of family violence, whenever we preach and teach we should correctly interpret these doctrines so that our people are empowered to resist the tyranny within their homes and gain liberation. The church must be on the side of the oppressed within its own families, rather than preaching oppression to the least of the members of the church family.[17]

In summary, some of our favorite Bible texts and interpretations sound false when we listen with the ears of victims and survivors of violence in black families. They may sound all right to adults who already feel empowered by church and society, but to those who are oppressed because of family violence, words like forgiveness, reconciliation, honor, headship, obedience, servanthood, and others often sound as if they further blame the victim rather than confront the perpetrator. Because the Bible is written to liberate those who are oppressed, we need to be careful with our words and interpretations.

There has been much work done to help the church reinterpret the Bible and revise its hymns and prayers in light of the needs and insights of victims and survivors of family violence. Kelly Brown Douglas suggests imaging Jesus as a black woman struggling for justice. "To portray Christ in the face of Black heroines and heroes signals that it was not who Jesus was, particularly as a male, that made him Christ, but what he did."[18] Jacquelyn Grant suggests an emphasis on discipleship, rather than servanthood, in order to empower women in families and in the church. Grant believes that discipleship as a symbol of faith in Jesus would lead to more equality between women and men, blacks and whites in the church and in society.[19] Delores Williams says that the image of Jesus as one who resists evil and promotes survival and liberation is more faithful to the religious witness of black women in the history of the black churches. Pastoral leaders must be familiar with the revised material that comes from scholars who give priority to the witness of victims and survivors of family violence.[20]

2. Work with Children and Youth

Because the role of the black church is predicated upon its historic witness and practice of being both the value giver and value guardian of the black community, the task of providing sex education and sexual norms for children and youth is crucial. This ministry is crucial because what black young people are taught about sexuality, and about the safety and well-being of their bodies, must match what they learn about the biblical understanding of how Jesus loves them—that they are indeed "precious in his sight"!

We know that over the next decades African American youth ministers will be confronted with two major challenges: to improve the development and dissemination of sex education and to impart this information adequately to a youth ministry population that is becoming increasingly sexually active and increasingly exposed to acts of violence at home as well as in the media.[21] Rap music that glorifies male physical violence against women and encourages sexual violence in rape and in acts of dominance that are humiliating and hurtful is rampant in African American youth culture. A further challenge lies in how sexuality education can incorporate the view of sexuality as a positive and integral part of faith development and experience while at the same time making adolescents aware of the negative consequences of sexual and domestic violence. Black ethicist and musician Garth Kasimu Baker-Fletcher has written eloquently on the subject of the role of the black church, black rap, and youth ministry. In a chapter entitled "Rap's 'Angry' Children," he challenges old forms of youth ministry with pointed questions:

> I believe it necessary to remind Christians that many of our churches are not places of liberating transcendence, but are the well-groomed halls of holy escapism. Within these walls we preach a message in which young men and women acquainted with the streets find it hard to discern any meaning or relevance. How can a young person who has witnessed the murder of a best friend, a lover, or a baby have any patience with a simplistic declaration of forgiveness and reconciliation? How can young folks whose lives are severely constricted and controlled by the flow of guns and drugs to support that "trade" find the boring reiteration of gospel pablum enough to feed their starving souls?[22]

From our experience as youth ministers, and from our research and dialogue with the teachers and leaders of young, gifted, and black people who are the future of the black church and the hope of the black community, we know that a more realistic approach to address the onslaught of violence that threatens their lives is so necessary. Ministers in the black community must offer more than choir, ushering, and antiseptic youth fellowships that deny the reality of violence, which so many black youth face daily, not only on the streets but in their homes and within their family history and daily existence. Baker-Fletcher continues:

We must brave the same dangers and foes as our children do every day if we are to expect them to listen and believe what we preach. The message of the gospel must deliberately find its way out onto those same killing streets that threaten the future of Afrikans, or young people will continue to smoke dope and get high, laughing at the gospel of Jesus Christ as the nonsense of weak-minded chumps.... If we challenge the streets in the safety of books, church services, and prayer meetings, we are not facing the evil, but running from it. The simple truth is that there is no safe place to be now. Either we stand up to such evil or be destroyed by its undermining, corrosive influence.[23]

Models of black youth ministry that directly or indirectly address the concerns of sexual and domestic violence are imaginatively available whenever we look directly at the young people who inhabit our churches. We draw upon the creativity of Trinity United Church of Christ, and its pastoral staff led by the Reverend Dr. Jeremiah Wright, for examples that work:[24]

Adopt a Student Ministry keeps the church in touch with those students who have gone away from home and are studying during the "fragile years" at universities and colleges out of the city and out of the state. Each ministry within the church adopts a student; sends a care package, tapes of the services, and letters or gifts; and stays in touch with that student through the school year. The primary purpose of this ministry is to let college students know that they do have a church home that cares about them.

Since the reality of date rape, the loneliness of being away from the values set by family and church family, and other small and large problems related to being in college can be better addressed by young people if there is a "family" member who is "in touch," this ministry can contribute to keeping violence to a minimum, even though it does not serve as a total prevention for the trials and difficulties of being alone and away from home.

Building Black Men is a Rites of Passage Program designed to develop black boys who have respect for African American women, who have respect for themselves, who have reverence and admiration for God, and who have a fierce commitment to the Church of Jesus Christ.

The graded programs start with youngsters who are eight years of age, and go all the way up through the pubescent years of thirteen to seventeen. A Rites of Passage ceremony is held annually for those students who complete the course. This exciting program takes part in the national Rites of Passage conferences held annually all over the country.

Building Black Women is a Rites of Passage Program for African American girls. The same principles utilized in the Building Black Men program are implemented here. Young women are taught to respect themselves first before seeking approval in the eyes and arms of others. They are taught to respect their community, to respect their bodies, to respect God, and to have a Christocentric view that is Afrocentric in origin.

A major accomplishment has been the completion of the "Sisterhood" quilt, a quilt of respect honoring African American heroines and women who have made indelible contributions to the life and history of African American people.

Dance Ministry is one of the most exciting ministries for young people in the church. It is composed of male and female liturgical dancers. The youth are taught the principles of modern ballet and interpretive dance. They are also taught the African roots of dance in worship and the biblical basis for praising God with the dance!

The monthly interpretations during the regular services of worship add a new dimension to the congregation's corporate prayer and inspire the young people to take their bodies—the gifts of God—more seriously and sacramentally.

3. Marriage Preparation and Weddings

Absent from most teaching about premarriage counseling and preparation for weddings has been awareness of family violence. There are at least three things that pastoral leaders in the black church must know as they work with couples preparing for marriage: the impact of childhood violence on the couple's relationship; the possibility of dating violence; and the danger signals about violence during marriage. Although we are talking specifically about heterosexual marriage in this section, many of the same principles apply to heterosexual couples who are living together and to gay and lesbian partners.

(1) Pastoral leaders in African American churches need to understand the impact of childhood violence on the couple's relationship. Research shows a high correlation between witnessing violent adults at home and engaging in violence as an adult in one's own relationship. This is because people learn from their experience. If a black child grows up watching a father or stepfather battering his or her mother, the child learns that such violence is a normal part of intimate adult relationships. Even though the child may hate the violence and be angry at the perpetrator, he or she may come to expect family violence in his or her own relationships. In many homes in which the father batters the mother, either the father or mother, or both, also beats the children. Even if a young adult planning to marry is not violent, he or she may not know healthy forms of intimate relationships. Emotional abuse that includes name calling, profanity, and degrading and threatening com-

ments can be very destructive even if there is no overt physical violence.

Because so many young African American adults have witnessed or personally experienced violence in their family of origin, pastoral leaders in the black church must be on the lookout for the impact of this violence in current relationships. By emphasizing that we learn what we live, a pastoral leader can suggest that, in spite of good intentions, the patterns that were painfully experienced as children will show up again in the relationships that the young adults are now establishing. The pastoral leader could give an example of a time he or she said something and was shocked that it sounded just like one of his or her parents. Many couples will not feel comfortable discussing in pre-marriage counseling their history of violence, but the fact that the pastoral leader mentioned it may help them to start thinking and may keep the door open for pastoral care many months or years later when they realize that the truth was spoken.

(2) Pastoral leaders in African American faith communities need to understand that dating violence is much more widespread than we have known until now. Research shows that some kind of physical violence, such as hitting or slapping, is in 20 to 50 percent of dating relationships.[25] Up to 37 percent of girls have experienced a rape or attempted rape during adolescence.[26] In addition, there is much emotional abuse as young people verbalize the negative attitudes they have learned from their families and the culture.

For example, many black young men use "bitch" to refer to their girlfriends as a matter of course. Many adolescent black girls report that they are forced or manipulated to engage in sexual activity when they are uncomfortable or would like to say no. The battering of girls and women is much more common in dating relationships than has been previously recognized. Pastoral leaders must be aware of the possibility of dating violence, mention it as a problem some couples face, and be prepared to intervene with a safety plan if the couple discloses the presence of violence in their current relationship.[27]

(3) In every premarriage counseling session, the pastoral leader of the black faith community should interpret the danger signs to the couple being counseled in case violence occurs in the future. If either partner of the couple has witnessed violence in her or his family of origin, or has experienced or perpetrated dating violence, then violence will likely reoccur during the marriage. But even for African American couples without any history of family violence, there is a possibility of violence between them or toward the children. The pastoral leader should make a clear ethical statement that battering of an intimate partner or physical or sexual abuse of children is wrong according to Christian teachings. Beyond that, the pastoral leader can educate the couple about the dangerous times when violence is likely to occur.

Violence is also likely during the first year of marriage after the honeymoon period wears off and conflict develops about sexuality; finances; work schedules; in-laws; extended family; previous children, relationships, or marriages; and the many everyday decisions that every couple needs to make. Violence is likely during pregnancy. Many battered African American women report that the first time they were beaten was when they became pregnant. Pregnancy makes a woman more vulnerable, and some husbands and boyfriends take advantage of this vulnerability to establish their dominance and control in the relationship. Violence is likely during illness, unemployment, onset of a disabling condition, a car accident—anything that disrupts the routine and makes one of the persons vulnerable to abuse in a new way.

Sometimes violence is first directed at the children and then becomes directed at the spouse. Sometimes the violence is sexual rather than physical. The molestation of young children is usually carried out in secret, and the spouse may not know the dreadful secret her child is hiding. Pastoral leaders in black faith communities should identify some of the danger signs and talk to the couple about resources available in the community, including hotline and shelter numbers.

4. Women's and Men's Groups

We have observed that congregational resources for safety and healing of domestic and sexual violence are available through the auspices and leadership of gender specific ministerial groups formed through the black church. Examples of such groups are readily apparent and not limited to the following working models:

Women's Fellowship: Following the traditional model of women in the black church who are concerned about healing and wholesome living with Christ at the center of their pilgrimage, the Women's Fellowship meets monthly, providing an outlet for women who seek to be more Christ-centered in their focus and to live up to their "oughtness" as Christian women in the church.

They serve in the heart of the community through relationships with agencies serving underprivileged, abused, and battered women and children.

Sisterhood: The Sisterhood is a group of married, single, divorced, widowed, young, and old Christian women who are dedicated to being all that God would have them be! This closely knit group of committed women has resulted in deeper faith convictions, healthier Christian walks, and more wholesome relationship building.

The testimonies of the women whose lives have been blessed by Sisterhood are "legion." This group represents those who had determined they would *never* be in a group with other women! Through Sisterhood they have found that myth exploded and have grown to be sisters truly in Christ. The opportunity to talk "women's talk," sharing struggles and sharing successes that include surviving sexual and domestic violence, is life-giving and health promoting.

In offering a form of pastoral care that he identifies as a "narrative approach," Edward P. Wimberly outlines a style that is rich with possibilities for the African American men's movement. He says that pastoral care with African American men emphasizes a holistic understanding of the maturing process of selfhood rooted in the deepest inner feelings, values, intentions, and spirituality emerging from a man's life.[28] He continues by adding pastoral counseling to pastoral care in ministries that enrich and heal the lives of black men:

> Through pastoral counseling, the African American male discovers his unique self, his true emotions and feelings, his meaning and purpose for life, and his unique contribution and vocation to the world. He is able to engage in all aspects of life, including the formation of close and intimate relationships with significant others, while taking full responsibility for his own growth and development. Pastoral counseling identifies the sources of his manhood as including his African heritage, the African American tradition of equalitarian relationships and androgynous roles, the penchant for oral styles of communication, the use of Bible stories and characters, and the capacity to be empathic with African American women.[29]

Men's Fellowship: Following the traditional model of men in the black church who are concerned about healthy and

wholesome living with Christ at the center of their pilgrimage, the Men's Fellowship meets monthly, providing an
outlet for men who seek to be more Christ-centered in their
focus and to discuss topics that affect the African American
Christian male in today's society.

5. Programs with Older Adults

Often pastoral leaders of African American faith communities are not used to thinking about family violence in
relation to older adults. Anne Streaty Wimberly, coordina-
tor of the Gerontology in Seminary Education Initiative at
the Interdenominational Theological Center in Atlanta, has
provided a wealth of information and education in her text,
*Honoring African American Elders: A Ministry in the Soul
Community.* She comments on the increasing reality of elder
abuse in the black community. Under the heading of "The
Practice of Honor-Bestowing Ministry," Stephen Rasor discusses the creation of elder ministries for different locations
and describes the problems and the possibilities of such a
ministry for the black church.

> Maltreated elders form a special subgroup of elders in
> which we find African Americans. Two points are of impor-
> tance with reference to them. First, elders who are abused
> do not necessarily acknowledge their abuse; nor do they
> always report it when they acknowledge it. This is because,
> typically, the abuser is a family member. But in our relations
> with elders, especially as part of a visitation ministry, we
> may see the effects of abuse. Second, abused elders often
> need encouragement to take necessary steps toward safety,
> and they need help in locating specialized psychosocial
> support personnel in order to address their situation.[30]

The black church has long taught its members about
respect for the "mothers of the church," honor of parents,
and the responsibility of the whole community to value the

wisdom of "the elders." The Afrocentric emphasis on respect for the ancestors who are watching over us gets translated into honor for older persons who are about to "pass over the Jordan into the promised land." Many of the most important leaders of African American churches are older adults who have real power to influence the ethos of the church community.

Research shows that elder abuse is a significant problem that has not received its due attention. Some studies estimate that 20 percent of elders experience some kind of physical, emotional, or sexual abuse within their extended families.[31] Given the values of the African American community, such statistics are shocking, and we may want to deny that this could happen.

Because there is secret abuse of elders going on in our black congregations and communities, our churches need to engage in education and pastoral care. One reason elder abuse is secret is because often we do not talk about it in the church. We recommend having workshops for the fellowship of older adults, led by a social worker in the community who understands and can provide insights into elder abuse and its prevention in the African American community.

6. Self-Help Groups

Many African American churches are centers for healing groups around specific interests. Some congregations even have their own treatment programs for drug and alcohol abuse and other problems. The twelve-step methods of Alcoholics Anonymous (AA) has been adapted to help people recover from eating disorders, gambling, compulsive spending, sexual addictions, and many other issues. In some churches there are groups for Parents Anonymous (persons who have been violent toward children), survivors of child sexual abuse, and men who have been violent toward women. We support the development of these groups and the congregations who acknowledge the traditional role of the church as a healing community.

However, we urge churches and pastoral leaders to use caution when linking these self-help groups to issues of family violence. Our caution is based on our previous motto: Safety for victims first. Any self-help group, regardless of beginning good motives, can become a place of danger if certain guidelines are not followed. First, persons who are in danger of family violence must have whatever anonymity and control they need to ensure their safety. This means that the time and meeting places of persons in immediate danger must be protected so that perpetrators will not seek them out for further threats. Second, such groups should be in close contact with professionals who have experience with the legal authorities and agencies in the community who can provide protection in times of extreme danger. Third, church leaders should be advised by professional experts and government agencies whenever they want to establish safe houses, shelters, or counseling programs for families experiencing abuse. The movement to protect and empower victims and survivors has made progress because it has learned from earlier mistakes. For example, there is a tendency for persons new to the field to underestimate the danger of perpetrators of family violence, and this misjudgment can result in permanent injury or murder of victims when they seek safety. It is possible that a well-intentioned program to provide resources for victims actually increases the danger that they will be killed when they seek help. Churches who decide to initiate support for victims must be informed and realistic about the difficulties of this task.

Another caution about self-help groups is that some of the twelve-step principles of AA do not work with family violence. The step that emphasizes loss of control is not appropriate for a perpetrator who has been using violence as a means of power and control. Most perpetrators need to be faced with consequences that force them to leave others alone and not hide behind the illusion that their violence is a loss of control. The step that emphasizes making right the wrongs to persons in the past can be used to justify further harassment of victims who fear any contact with the perpetrator. Also, an emphasis on alcohol or drug abuse as the primary diagnosis of one's problems can be used to hide the equally or more serious problem of violence against vulnerable persons. AA and NA (Narcotics Anonymous) do not adequately deal with the violence of perpetrators within the family. This lapse in understanding can be used to deny or minimize the consequences of one's violence for the safety and lives of others.

For these reasons, we urge caution in the use of self-help groups and principles when applied to issues of family violence. When self-help groups are organized with full understanding of the principles of healing for families experiencing abuse, especially the principle of Safety First, then these groups can be helpful resources. If the principles we have outlined in this book are ignored, self-help groups can be sites of further danger and exploitation of those who are vulnerable.

7. Community Outreach Ministries

Prison Ministry: "When I was in prison you visited me." The words of Jesus provide the impetus for this dedicated group of persons who volunteer their time every week of the year! Fifty-two times a year the prison ministers are in the jails and prisons working with incarcerated individuals in every level of ministry. They do tutorial work, teaching inmates how to read, how to do math, and how to increase their word usage in composition skills. In addition to the inmates, they work with the families of inmates.

We know that violence begets violence and that many persons incarcerated in the criminal justice system are there because of appropriate or inappropriate responses to the domestic and sexual violence they have known in their lives as children or as adults. This ministry is a means of healing the trauma and terror of this reality, which has brought so many African American men and women to be hopelessly caught in a prison system which serves only to dehumanize them further.

> *Foster Care Ministry:* Members of the church who themselves are foster care parents or who work with the various foster care programs of the city and state, and who have a deep and abiding interest in seeing that every child has a safe and healthy home, make up the constituency of this vital ministry.

Through their caring and labor, black families can offer outreach to the numerous battered and abused children who desperately need a loving home environment. Being advocates for abandoned and orphaned black children and monitoring the system of foster care so that abuse does not occur within it are also a part of this ministry to child victims of domestic and sexual abuse.

> *Legal Counseling Ministry:* Lawyers of the church volunteer their time and tithe their talents by providing free legal counseling to members of the church and by doing several more minor tasks (like preparing wills for senior citizens) pro bono as a part of their ministry to the suffering and victimized Body of Christ.

They also organize a network and support group for young law students who are in the process of becoming lawyers. They perform an invaluable service to the members of the congregation whose entanglement with the law, because of complications in divorce cases, legal orders to keep violent intimate partners away, and other legal negotiations necessary for their safety and survival, require expert legal advice.

8. Ethics for Churches and Pastoral Leaders

Parental authority is granted in order that parents may love and nurture their children toward physical, emotional, and spiritual wholeness. The very idea of the family is based on the assumption that the love of a family is an ideal place for children to grow up with high self-esteem and a love of God and people. The privacy of adults who live together in intimate relationships by marriage or custom is granted by society because love needs privacy to thrive. We assume that two persons in love will treat each other with respect and care and will negotiate their relationship in a way that encourages both to grow into their full potential as children of God.

Family violence is an abuse of the power that has been given by society to parents and persons in intimate relationships. When black parents beat or molest their children, they betray the trust of society that their parental power will be used for the benefit of children. Children are not possessions but gifts of God for parents to love and respect, so that they can become the adults God intends them to be. Violence destroys children so they become walking wounded. When black adults batter their partners in marriage or partnership, they betray the public promises they made to love and respect this person "'til death do us part." Partner violence is a violation of the covenant between a couple and the community and between a couple and the church. When this covenant is broken, the victim has a right to bring a complaint and make appeal to the church, and the church must be willing to listen because it was a party to the covenant. The reason we make such covenants at baby dedications, baptisms, marriages, and accepting partners into the church is because we know black family life is often difficult and couples and families need the supportive nurture and expectations of how they should behave. When the covenant is broken, victims should be encouraged to come before the church and ask for redress, and the black church should respond appropriately.

If the black church is to fulfill its calling as a sanctuary for children and adults experiencing abuse, then the church must examine its own uses and abuses of power. This is the question of ethics: do the church and its leaders live up to their covenants between God and the people about the use of power? We raise this question here because a church that abuses its power cannot help families in which there is an abuse of power. The church that is unethical in the way it treats people will not have the ethical standing to call its families to account. Too often family violence is a mirror of the unethical ways that people in the church treat one another. If we expect our families to respect the integrity of every person and refrain from the use of violence and abusive behaviors, then we must call the church community and its leaders to have integrity in uses of power.[32]

Summary

In this chapter, we have extended the principles of pastoral care for African American families experiencing abuse to discussion of congregational models and strategies that will help to educate our people about family violence. What we have written is only the beginning of a longer discussion needed in the churches about black family violence. We believe that family violence has implications that affect many areas of the black church's life and program, including the use of the Bible in preaching and worship, and the ethical standards that guide our leaders in their uses of power. We have made suggestions, which we hope will inform the churches as they discuss issues of family violence, and we encourage a spirited and serious debate about these issues for the health of the whole people of God.

Chapter Nine

Concluding Ethical Reflections

There is a balm in Gilead, to make the wounded whole,
There is a balm in Gilead, to heal the sin-sick soul.

Sometimes I feel discouraged, and think my work's in vain,
But then the Holy Spirit revives my soul again.

Don't ever feel discouraged, For Jesus is your friend,
And if you look for knowledge, He'll ne'er refuse to lend.

If you cannot preach like Peter, if you cannot pray like Paul,
You can tell the love of Jesus, And say "He died for all."[1]

We began this volume, which focuses on pastoral care for African American families experiencing abuse, by asking the question, Who needs a balm for Gilead? In employing the verses of the traditional African American spiritual, "Balm in Gilead," we have deliberately evoked memories of the famed healing ointment, referred to in the Bible, which was prized for its therapeutic and medicinal qualities. The fabled balm and the famous physician of Gilead, mentioned in Jeremiah 8:22 and 46:11, were sought after to cure the children of Israel, as well as the children of Egypt, from death-dealing ills.

'Harvest is over, summer at an end
and we have not been saved!'
The wound of the daughter of my people wounds me too,
all looks dark to me, terror grips me.
Is there not a balm in Gilead any more?

Is no doctor there?
Then why is there no progress
in the cure of the daughter of my people?
Who will turn my head into a fountain,
and my eyes into a spring for tears,
that I can weep day and night,
over the slain of the daughter of my people?
                    (Jeremiah 8:20-23, italics added)

Go up to Gilead and fetch balm,
virgin daughter of Egypt!
You multiply remedies in vain,
nothing can cure you!
The nations have heard of your shame,
your wailing fills the world,
for warrior has stumbled against warrior,
and both have fallen together.
                    (Jeremiah 46:11-12, italics added)

We have reviewed the stark realities and the pastoral and prophetic roles of the black family, which functions as a domestic church,[2] in responding to the violence and the pain that fills the lives of so many of its members. We have sought to establish and link theological, sociological, and pastoral relationships between the institutions of the black family and the black church. We believe and have sought to show that a healing remedy is readily available and accessible through the pastoral care resources and auspices of the black and believing faith community, in its victims and survivors, and in its religious leaders who serve as both value givers and guardians.

We know that the healers of Gilead in the black community are actively engaged in resisting the evil of sexual abuse and in restoring the health, well-being, and self-esteem of the children and families who have suffered intolerably from the incredibly debilitating and diabolical effects engendered by domestic violence. In this concluding chapter we offer a closing commentary in support of the ethic of care[3] that is so necessary to maintain the health and life of black families, as well as their pastoral care givers and religious leaders, and to model the justice-love ethic of the gospel for all those affected by the evils of sexual violence and domestic abuse.

Research and writing on an ethic of care have become "a minor academic industry"[4] concerning the nature of the human person; the roles of personality and environment, especially social environment in human behavior; the developmental aspects of human life; and especially the specific impact of race and ethnicity, gender, and class. Many of these areas of research have undergone vast perspectival changes over the past twenty-five years, whether undertaken in philosophy, psychology, educational theory, or religious studies. Nonetheless, the theology of pastoral care that we have proposed is based on a prior commitment to an ethos of biblically based justice that is congruent with black Christian love.[5]

This perspective distinguishes our ethic of care from that of many mainstream feminist models[6] representing this approach, and directs our concluding recommendations toward a model that is specifically oriented to addressing a future full of hope that will last for black families and the black church as these institutions evolve and renew themselves. By an ethic of care established and espoused by black families who are agents and images of the domestic black church, we mean to emphasize a liberational ethos,

> which is regularly practiced and embodied by black women [and men]. I do not suggest this ethic involves and identifies burdened representatives of what is pejoratively understood as "women's work." Rather it is evidenced in the lives of those mothers and moral agents of the race whose self-initiated expressions of care have undergirded the survival of a people. They have indeed secured a future

legacy that is humane, holistic, and compassionate for all who chose to belong to their unfolding and liberating extended families.[7]

By articulating an ethic of care for pastoral care givers within the black church, for black family members, and for all those who strive to be in solidarity with them, we also mean to describe and delineate an ethos that sustains a praxis that challenges and changes any sexual ethic that overlooks or understates the reality of sexual violence in the church and the community. Along with Marie Fortune and others,[8] whose research and work on sexual violence have confronted all complacent forms of pastoral ministry, we are well aware that

> Sexual violence as a topic for ethical discourse among Christians has gone unaddressed. There are many complex reasons for this. One reason is certainly the silence on the topic by society as a whole. Ethicists and pastors, like judges, doctors, police officers, and the general public have paid little attention to the problem of sexual violence. Specifically in the Christian community, rape and child sexual abuse have been largely overlooked by most ethicists who have shaped traditional and contemporary ethical discussion.[9]

By an ethic of care applicable to victims and survivors of violence and abuse in black families, who turn to the black church and other agencies of social service, social justice, and social change for provision as well as protection, we signal four insights, which form the core of a pastoral praxis that is as evangelical as it is effective in offering "Good News" to those who are oppressed. We also will summarize some principles of sexual ethics that may apply to male pastoral leaders in the black faith community.

Ethical Insights That Address Root Causes of Domestic Violence in the African American Community

- *The first ethical insight is a call to renew faith as both belief and action*

Our first ethical insight calls for a praxis of truth telling, of naming the violence. In an oral, womanist collection of folk proverbs known as Mama Said's, we find a proverb often quoted in the black community, "Every shut eye ain't sleep!" Because the black community, and particularly the black religious community, is well aware of the instances of domestic violence and sees it even if it does not readily want to talk about it, especially in church, we are called to action, for we know that we are not asleep. We are called to keep company with the Guardian God of Israel who neither slumbers nor sleeps in vigil over a beloved black community.

This first insight is a call to be converted from what Stephen Carter, an African American legal scholar at Yale, writes about as indolence in his important work, *The Culture of Disbelief.* This work is an analysis of the character of contemporary American culture that deems it politically incorrect to let faith or religion publicly influence national debate and reflection.

In this work, Carter makes the claim that religious convictions, like religious institutions and their personnel, are being marginalized by media and culture into "appropriate" Sunday slots. The American Christian community, including the black community, internalizes this indolence and marginalization by not allowing faith to influence the discussions of the whole week.[10] We make the claim that this is true especially in the case of domestic violence and sexual misconduct of black men, and of the clergy in particular. Carter's work is a call to all womanists, men and women alike, to speak up and to speak out on the endemic problem in the black community; to renew the conscious link between our belief and action; to protect black women and children from physical harm (a historically liberating praxis from preslavery eras); and to shelter the widow and the orphan and the stranger (a biblical injunction from Deuteronomy 10:14-19, 24:17-22, and 27:19 that has been taken seriously by the extended black family model and that has been operative up until contemporary times).

- *The second ethical insight is the restoration of self-respect as an indispensable element in our abilities to conquer the environment of violence in the black community.*

In black colloquial and proverbial parlance again, we invoke the song of Aretha Franklin, "R-E-S-P-E-C-T!" Ralph Willey, in his collection of essays entitled, *Why Black People Tend to Shout*, attempts an analysis of the mind-set of many underclass black men. His review of the movie *Boys 'n the Hood* makes it clear that the absence of positive images in film and life are creating only violent alternatives for black men's responses to their hopeless situation.[11] George Bernard Shaw noted that poverty does not produce unhappiness; it produces degradation. Degradation is an illness of soul, a product of negative self-perception that yields hopelessness. We observe that degradation is dissipated by the balm of self-respect and self-esteem which the black church is so capable of bestowing on those who are weak, frail, and without hope except for this protective and proactive ecclesial presence.

In his book *Rethinking the American Race Problem*, Roy L. Brooks calls attention to a quality among underclass, violence-prone males called "sorriness."[12] It is a kind of extended adolescence affecting some African American boys and men suffering from a history of subordination. It differs from the white psychological experience of extended adolescence known as the "Peter Pan syndrome" in that its victims face the prospect of long-term poverty, prison, physical injury, or even death if there is no person or group such as the functional black family or church or community to pick up the pieces.

The point here is that the lack of attention we pay to issues of self-worth among underclass people and people historically abused by repeated experiences of subordination confirms structures of hopelessness, which generate violent reactions to the environment. The proverb of traditional African religion, "I am because we are," and the African American proverb "I am Somebody!"[13] are important reflections and realizations, which invite and require black pastoral and ethical response, particularly response to issues of domestic violence and abuse for both women and men.

- *The third ethical insight calls for transformation of social structures that manifest sin.*

In the parlance of a Mama Said proverb, we know that "God don't like ugly—ugly is as ugly does." This womanist-inspired theological and ethical comment on social sin suggests that the culture of violence in which we find ourselves globally situated calls us beyond private escapism to a spirituality based on challenging oppressive and dysfunctional social structures. Global military violence, in which the United States participates on a regular basis, is an analogy to the domestic violence that so many African American men unwittingly mimic in the privacy of their family homes and church homes where it is imperative that they be "in charge"—or else.

Stephen Carter's work again reminds us of the admonitions that Alexis de Tocqueville advanced in his consideration of the role of religions in a democratic society.[14] First, religions are the source of moral understanding avoiding deterioration into simple tyranny. The black church must be a source of moral understanding that can help violent and abusive black men avoid turning into tyrannical and violent dictators in the home and in the public arenas where they exercise particular influence over young children, female adolescents, and women.

Second, religions, in Carter's view, are responsible for mediation between citizens and the apparatus of government, providing an independent moral voice.[15] Carter suggests that religious people must form those associations that by the strength of faith and praxis provide a voice for the voiceless. The voices of individuals and groups like Marian Wright Edelman and the Children's Defense Fund[16] are models for the kind of powerful political influence that the black church must cultivate more intentionally when it chooses to act as a prophetic mediator between citizens and the apparatus of government, providing an independent moral voice that echoes the prophetic voices and deeds of our biblical heritage.

- *The fourth and final ethical insight calls for an inclusive ethic of black Christian love for all individuals and congregations, regardless of the conditions of birth, sexual preference, or previous engagement in expressions of domestic violence either as an abuser or a victim.*

We have cited an ethic of "black love" as an indispensable element of pastoral care for African American families experiencing abuse, an ethic which calls for a justice-love that is inclusive of all. This ethic of black love specifically requires that relationships model the compassion and acceptance of a God who is with us to liberate us from all forms of violence, especially those that have roots in the brutal oppressiveness of misogyny, pedophilia, and homophobia.

We affirm that black love is the agent of gospel liberation as well as the strongest asset of the black and believing community. Black love, expressed through the faithful witness of African American spirituality and sexuality, creates awareness of the living God who is in every place. We claim that black love sustains the ability of the black faith community to choose and discern, and nurtures the sense of bonding that allows black women and men to be distinctive in their style of self-acceptance. Black love confirms and affirms the community's affection for God, self, and others, especially those who have also been oppressed.

In an earlier chapter we indicated how the roots of sexual violence and domestic abuse found their way into the social institution of the black family through its heritage of a violent slave history. We repeat this reflection on black love here in order to indicate how this ethic, like a balm for Gilead, has worked incessantly to heal the unfortunate effects of this violent past:

> Historically, it was criminal for blacks to express extended love for one another or to establish lasting relationships of social interdependence and care. Blacks were wrenched from our African societies in which sexual behavior was orderly and firm under family and community controls. Under the system of slavery black people were bred like animals; white men were allowed to sexually coerce and abuse black women; black families were frequently broken up and legal marriage was often prohibited. Sexual instability was forced upon the African American community.
>
> Racist myths and stereotypes perpetuated these distortions to this day, falsely detailing black hypersexual activity and an inability to maintain and nurture marital commitments. Racists also repeat ubiquitous rumors about untrue violent relationships among black men and their women or wives. It is impossible for the many white Americans reared on this pathological mythology to think, speak, or write with historical accuracy or ethical understanding about the integrity of authentic, real black love and relationships.
>
> Despite these assaults, black love has continuously flowed between black people, almost like a breath ...breathing life into dead situations. This death-defying capacity of black women and men to go on giving and receiving love has been incredibly preserved in spite of a hostile and racist American environment. Such tenacious black love had its spiritual genesis in African soil where it developed unencumbered, at least in its beginnings, by the prejudices of American puritanical Christianity.[17]

We must hold onto this strong ethical inheritance of black love from our African past if there is to be any hope for nurturance, growth, and fruitfulness in black family relationships in our black church and community. We believe the responsibility for encouraging and promoting black love as a balm for African American families experiencing abuse depends largely on pastoral leadership. Over centuries, the black church has granted authority to black pastors to identify and protect the community from white racism and to provide moral leadership for the internal ethic of families, congregations, and the larger black community. When this pastoral authority is misused to exploit those who are vulnerable within the black community, the moral integrity of the whole community is jeopardized. Therefore we call for renewed discussion of accountability for the exercise of all authority within the black community, whether parents over children, the strong over the weak, intimate partners against each other, pastors over congregations. In order to deal with domestic violence as an issue of black love, the black community must be willing to reexamine all authority, whether from God or from humans.

The ethical insights and principles listed above form the core and center of our hope and belief that there is a balm for Gilead.[18] We are convinced that defining and redefining an ethic of care for African American families experiencing abuse is a principal task as well as a covenantal commitment of those who are called to lead and serve in the black church. We believe that ways of knowing, learning, and making moral choices must become a principal agenda for those centers of theological education and seminary formation, which are responsible for training future religious leaders to be ministers skilled and astute in preventing family violence and for healing atrocities caused by abuse and lack of care. We continue to work in solidarity with pastors, civic and social representatives, and others concerned about supporting public political agendas that make a difference to those black family members who have been devastated by the failures of religion and society to provide relief from the suffering and stigma of sexual violation and physical pain.

The enduring legacy of African American families experiencing abuse is one of immeasurable resistance to unimaginable evil. The lasting testament of black and believing families is one of unceasing resilience in the face of incredible odds calculated to make even the most optimistic among us falter. The poignantly moving stories of the victims and survivors who have contributed to this text cause us to give thanks for the power of faith and the richness of authentic black love that is so evident in their witness and willingness to share their life stories so that others might benefit from their pain. We take solace and sustenance from hearing and believing, and from attempting to live out with others the stirring strains of that traditional sacred tune, which is sung repeatedly and confidently by mothers and fathers, pastors, teachers, and preachers in the black church and community to their children, to their abusers, and for all those who work unceasingly to bring an end to violence in all its forms.

There is a balm in Gilead, to make the wounded whole,
There is a balm in Gilead, to heal the sin-sick soul.

Sometimes I feel discouraged, and think my work's in vain,
But then the Holy Spirit revives my soul again.

Don't ever feel discouraged, For Jesus is your friend,
And if you look for knowledge, He'll ne'er refuse to lend.

If you cannot preach like Peter, if you cannot pray like Paul,
You can tell the love of Jesus, And say "He died for all."[19]

NOTES

Introduction

1. This description draws heavily on the statement of purpose of the Center for the Prevention of Sexual and Domestic Violence. We are grateful for our ongoing association with the Center and its director, the Reverend Marie M. Fortune. See *Violence Against Women and Children: A Christian Theological Sourcebook*, ed. Carol J. Adams and Marie M. Fortune (New York: Continuum, 1995), 504.

2. We derive our understanding of and context for our use of the term *womanist* from a variety of sources that have relevance for this study of abuse within black families. See Toinette M. Eugene, "Womanist Theology," in *New Handbook of Christian Theology*, ed. Donald Musser and Joseph Price (Nashville: Abingdon Press, 1992), 510-12; James Newton Poling, *Deliver Us from Evil: Resisting Racial and Gender Oppression* (Minneapolis: Fortress, 1996), 89-91; Katie G. Cannon, *Black Womanist Ethics* (Atlanta: Scholars Press, 1989); Jacquelyn Grant, *White Women's Christ, Black Women's Jesus: Feminist Christology and Womanist Response* (Atlanta: Scholars, 1989); Emilie Townes, *Womanist Justice, Womanist Hope* (Atlanta: Scholars Press, 1993); Kelly Brown Douglas, *The Black Christ* (Maryknoll, N.Y.: Orbis, 1994); and Delores Williams, *Sisters in the Wilderness: The Challenge of Womanist God-Talk* (Maryknoll, N.Y.: Orbis, 1993).

3. The praxis wheel is a methodology of liberation theology and social ethics that we regularly employ in our classes and that uses the insights and skills of social science, social ethics, liberation theology, and biblical exegesis in order to arrive at a praxis grounded in prayerful reflection and faithful community action. See Joe Holland and Peter Henriot, S.J., *Social Analysis: Linking Faith and Justice*, revised and enlarged edition (Maryknoll, N.Y.: Orbis, 1983).

4. James Newton Poling, *Deliver Us from Evil: Resisting Racial and Gender Oppression* (Minneapolis: Fortress, 1996), 129.

5. We recognize the pioneering research and writing of Edward P. Wimberly in his groundbreaking work, *Pastoral Care in the Black Church* (Nashville: Abingdon Press, 1979). We have been instructed and informed by the innovative and imaginative pastoral model of Jeremiah A. Wright Jr. at Trinity United Church of Christ in Chicago, where we have worshiped and have learned from the ministers and programs of this extraordinary congregation.

1. The Black Church and the Black Family

1. J. Deotis Roberts, *Roots of a Black Future: Family and Church* (Philadelphia: Westminster, 1980), 108.

2. See Robert L. Hampton, ed., *Violence in the Black Family: Correlates and Consequences* (Lexington, Mass.: Lexington Books, 1987). To date, this is the most

systematic and sustained scholarly review of violence as it is experienced within the African American community. Other texts which offer salient and sobering social analysis are: James P. Comer, M.D., and Alvin F. Poussaint, M.D., *Raising Black Children* (New York: Plume, 1992); Nathan Hare and Julia Hare, *The Endangered Black Family: Coping with the Unisexualization and Coming Extinction of the Black Race* (San Francisco: Black Think Tank, 1984); Lee N. June, ed., *The Black Family: Past, Present, and Future: Perspectives of Sixteen Black Christian Leaders* (Grand Rapids: Zondervan Publishing House, 1991), see in particular the essay by Joan A. Ganns, "Sexual Abuse: Its Impact on the Child and the Family," 173-86; Robert Staples and Leanor Boulin Johnson, *Black Families at the Crossroads: Challenges and Prospects* (San Francisco: Jossey-Bass, 1993).

3. Beth Richie-Bush, "Facing Contradictions: Challenge for Black Feminists," in *Aegis*, as quoted in Evelyn C. White, "Life Is a Song Worth Singing: Ending Violence in the Black Family," in *Working Together to Prevent Sexual and Domestic Violence* 5 (November-December 1984): 2.

4. Toinette M. Eugene, "The Black Family That Is Church," in *Families Black and Catholic—Catholic and Black*, ed. Thea Bowman (Washington: United States Catholic Conference, 1985), 54-60.

5. J. Deotis Roberts, *Roots of a Black Future: Family and Church* (Philadelphia: Westminster, 1980).

6. Olin P. Moyd, *Redemption in Black Theology* (Valley Forge: Judson, 1979), 199.

7. Roberts, *Roots of a Black Future,* 11. Italics added.

8. Ibid.

9. See Toinette M. Eugene, "African American Family Life: An Agenda for Ministry Within the Catholic Church," *New Theology Review* 5 (May 1992): 2.

10. John Paul II, *Familiaris Consortio: Regarding the Role of the Christian Family in the Modern World* (Washington D.C.: United States Catholic Conference), 46.

11. Roberts, *Roots of a Black Future*, 8.

12. J. Deotis Roberts, "The Black Church's Ministry to Families: Priestly Ministry," in *Black Theology Today: Liberation and Contextualization* (New York: Edwin Mellon, 1983).

13. Wallace Charles Smith, *The Church in the Life of the Black Family* (Valley Forge: Judson, 1985).

14. Ibid., 13, 74.

15. Ibid., 24.

16. Ibid., 34-40, 55, 59-62.

17. Ibid., 85ff.

18. Henry Mitchell and Nicholas Cooper Lewter, *Soul Theology: The Heart of American Black Culture* (San Francisco: Harper and Row, 1986).

19. Ibid., 168.

20. Wade Nobles and Lawford L. Goddard, "Black Family Life: A Theoretical and Policy Implication Literature Review," in *The Black Family: An Afrocentric Perspective*, ed. Aminifu R. Harvey (New York: United Church of Christ Commission for Racial Justice, 1985), 25-89.

21. W. E. B. DuBois, *The Philadelphia Negro* (1899; reprint, New York: Schocken Books, 1967), 201. Italics added.

22. In Gutman's unsurpassed historical treatise, *The Black Family in Slavery and Freedom, 1750-1925* (New York: Pantheon Books, 1976), he definitively cites the presence of the black family in both its monogamic and polygamic forms in the United States preceding the advent of what we understand to be the formation of the black Christian church. See pp. 90f., n. 26, for clarification of this matter con-

tradicted by the scholarship of W. E. B. DuBois not only in *The Philadelphia Negro,* but also in his *The Souls of Black Folk* (Greenwich: Fawcett, 1961), 145.

23. Hart M. Nelsen, Raytha L. Yokley, and Anne K. Nelsen, *The Black Church in America* (New York: Basic Books, 1971), 3.

24. C. Eric Lincoln, *The Black Church Since Frazier* (New York: Schocken Books, 1974), 116.

25. Ibid., 115.

26. C. Eric Lincoln, *The Black Experience in Religion* (Garden City, N.Y.: Anchor Books, 1974), 3.

27. See Gayraud S. Wilmore and James H. Cone, eds., *Black Theology: A Documentary History, 1966-1979* (Maryknoll, N.Y.: Orbis, 1979), 241.

28. Daniel C. Thompson, *Sociology of the Black Experience* (Westport, Conn.: Greenwood Press, 1974), 124.

29. Robert Staples, *Introduction to Black Sociology* (New York: McGraw-Hill, 1976), 166.

30. Ibid.

31. Lyrics for "Balm in Gilead" as they appear in *Songs of Zion* (Nashville: Abingdon Press, 1981), 123.

2. The Context of Oppression and Abuse for African American Families

1. Andrew Billingsley and Amy Tate Billingsley, *Black Families in White America* (Prentice-Hall, 1968), 68-69.

2. Herbert G. Gutman, *The Black Family in Slavery and Freedom, 1750-1925* (New York: Pantheon Books, 1976); Jacqueline Jones, *Labor of Love, Labor of Sorrow: Black Women, Work, and the Family from Slavery to the Present* (New York: Vintage, 1985). Jones's work, winner of both the Bancroft Prize and the Brown Publication Prize of the Association of Black Women Historians, has been hailed as "a seminal work of scholarship, which has no rival in its subtle explication of the complex interface of work, sex, race, and class" (Henry Louis Gates). This historic text illuminates and sustains the import of our present chapter on oppressions and the ways in which the work of womanists opens us to new directions for resisting the evil of violence and abuse within African American family (domestic church) systems and structures.

3. Alan P. Bell, "Black Sexuality: Fact and Fancy," in *The Black Family: Essays and Studies,* 2d ed., ed. Robert Staples (Belmont, Calif.: Wadsworth Publishing Company, 1978), 77-80.

4. Ida B. Wells-Barnett, "How Enfranchisement Stops Lynching," in *Ida B. Wells-Barnett: An Exploratory Study of An American Black Woman, 1893-1930,* ed. Mildred I. Thompson (Brooklyn: Carlson Publishing, 1990), 267-76.

5. See Patricia Morton, *Disfigured Images: The Historical Assault on Afro-American Women* (New York: Praeger, 1991), who cites a prominent white historian's assertion that "it was actually in large part because of the ex-slave woman's now uncontrolled wantonness that the black man turned from her in disgust to pursue women of the white race—and thus to the horrible crime of rape," 28.

6. See Nancie Caraway, *Segregated Sisterhood: Racism and the Politics of American Feminism* (Knoxville: University of Tennessee Press, 1991), especially chapter 5, "Gender Tyranny: Coded Bodies, Femininity, and Black Womanhood."

7. Nancy Boyd-Franklin, *Black Families in Therapy: A Multisystems Approach* (New York: Guilford, 1989), 7-9.

8. Elmer Martin and Joanne Mitchell Martin, *The Black Extended Family* (Chicago: University of Chicago Press, 1978), 93.

9. Ibid., 1.

10. Milton Sernett, *Afro-American Religious History: A Documentary Witness* (Durham: Duke University Press, 1985), 13-14.

11. See ibid., 19ff. See also Zora Neale Hurston, *Tell My Horse* (New York: J. B. Lipponcott, 1938), for other descriptions of African religious practices that have survived into the twentieth century. See W. W. Nobles, "Africanity: Its Role in Black Families," *The Black Scholar* 5 (1974): 10-17, and J. S. Mbiti, *African Religions and Philosophies* (Garden City, N.Y.: Anchor, 1969).

12. For an alternative interpretation of the spiritualism of the New Testament, see Walter Wink, *Naming the Powers: The Language of Power in the New Testament* (Philadelphia: Fortress, 1984).

13. C. Eric Lincoln and Lawrence H. Mamiya, *The Black Church in the African American Experience* (Durham, Duke University Press, 1990), 2, 7.

14. Gutman, *The Black Family*, xxi.

15. Boyd-Franklin, *Black Families in Therapy*, 9-10.

16. Ibid., 10.

17. For further discussion of these related ideas see Toinette M. Eugene, "While Love Is Unfashionable: Ethical Implications of Black Spirituality and Sexuality," in *Sexuality and the Sacred: Sources for Theological Reflection*, ed. James B. Nelson and Sandra P. Longfellow (Louisville: Westminster/John Knox, 1994), 106-11.

18. Jacquelyn Grant, "Black Theology and the Black Woman," in *Black Theology: a Documentary History, 1966-1979*, ed. Gayraud Wilmore and James Cone (Maryknoll, N.Y.: Orbis, 1979), 422.

19. Ibid.

20. James B. Nelson has made extensive use of the concepts of sexist and spiritualistic dualism in *Embodiment: An Approach to Sexuality and Christian Theology* (New York: Pilgrim, 1976). See especially chapter 3. We have attempted to turn his categories into explicit reflections on black sexual experience.

21. See John Mbiti, *The Prayers of African Religion* (New York: Orbis, 1975), and his *Concepts of God in Africa* (London: SPCK, 1970), for further connections made on the nexus between black spirituality and an integral worldview.

22. See Rosemary Radford Ruether, *New Woman, New Earth: Sexist Ideologies and Human Liberation* (New York: Seabury, 1975), chapter 5.

23. Grant, "Black Theology and the Black Woman," 422.

24. Eldridge Cleaver, as quoted by Robert Bellah in *The Broken Covenant: American Civil Religion in Time of Trial* (New York: Seabury, 1975), 105.

25. See Victoria King, *Manhandled Black Females* (Nashville: Winston-Derek, 1992); Patricia Morton, *Disfigured Images: The Historical Assault on Afro-American Women* (New York: Praeger, 1991); and Melba Wilson, *Crossing the Boundary: Black Women Survive Incest* (Seattle: Seal Press, 1993).

26. Robert L. Hampton, "Violence Against Black Children: Current Knowledge and Future Research Needs," in *Violence in the Black Family: Correlates and Consequences*, ed. Robert L. Hampton (Lexington, Mass.: Lexington Books, 1987), 4.

27. Ibid., 3.

28. Ibid., 24.

29. Ibid., 6.

30. See Hampton, *Violence in the Black Family*, 4-5.

31. James Garabino and Aaron Ebata, "The Significance of Ethnic and Cultural Differences in Child Maltreatment," in *Violence in the Black Family,* ed. Robert L. Hampton, 21f.

32. Hampton, "Violence Against Black Children," in *Violence in the Black Family,* ed. Hampton, 3.

33. Garabino and Ebata, "The Significance of Ethnic and Cultural Differences," in *Violence in the Black Family,* ed. Hampton, 23.

34. Robert L. Hampton, "Family Violence and Homicides in the Black Community: Are They Linked?" in *Violence in the Black Family,* ed. Hampton, 149.

35. Darnell F. Hawkins, "Devalued Lives and Racial Stereotypes: Ideological Barriers to the Prevention of Family Violence among Blacks," in *Violence in the Black Family,* ed. Robert L. Hampton, 192.

36. Angela Davis, *Women, Race, and Class* (New York: Random House, 1983), 13.

37. Angela Davis, *Women, Culture, and Politics* (New York: Random House, 1990), 77.

38. Hampton, "Family Violence and Homicides," in *Violence in the Black Family,* ed. Hampton, 153.

39. James P. Comer, "Black Violence and Public Policy: Changing Directions," in *American Violence and Public Policy,* ed. Lynn Curtis (New Haven: Yale University Press, 1985), 63-86.

40. Ibid., 65-66.

41. Alice Walker, *The Third Life of Grange Copeland* (New York: Harcourt Brace, 1970), 55.

42. Pat Parker, cited by Pam Annas in "As Common as the Best of Bread: Judy Grahn, Pat Parker, and Working Class Poetry," *New Lesbian Writiny,* ed. Margaret Cruikshank (San Francisco: Grey Fox, 1984), 113.

3. Defining Abuse in African American Families

1. Beth Richie-Bush, "Facing Contradictions: Challenge for Black Feminists," *Aegis* 37 (1983): 16.

2. Mary Lystad, ed., *Violence in the Home* (New York: Brunner/Mazel, 1986); Lloyd Ohlin and Michael Tonry, eds., *Family Violence* (Chicago: University of Chicago Press, 1989); and Dante Cicchetti and Vicki Carlson, eds., *Child Maltreatment* (New York: Cambridge University Press, 1989).

3. Robert L. Hampton, ed., *Violence in the Black Family: Correlates and Consequences* (Lexington, Mass.: Lexington Books, 1987).

4. Hampton, "Violence Against Black Children: Current Knowledge and Future Research Needs," in *Violence in the Black Family,* ed. Hampton, 3.

5. See Melba Wilson, *Crossing the Boundary: Black Women Survive Incest* (Seattle: Seal, 1993); Victoria King, *Manhandled Black Females* (Nashville: Winston-Derek, 1992).

6. Evelyn C. White, *Chain, Chain, Change: For Black Women Dealing with Physical and Emotional Abuse* (Seattle: Seal, 1985), 64.

7. See Hampton, *Violence in the Black Family;* and James P. Comer, "Black Violence and Public Policy: Changing Directions," in *American Violence and Public Policy,* ed. Lynn Curtis (New Haven: Yale University Press, 1985).

8. We are mindful of Ronald Reagan's and others' caricature of "the welfare queen" who drives in a limousine to get her check from the government, and of

George Bush's television advertisements about Willie Horton, the prisoner who was released on furlough from a Massachusetts prison and committed another crime. The media's preoccupation with drugs, guns, and homicides in the cities is another way in which public fears about black violence are fanned.

9. A model for this approach can be found in White, *Chain, Chain, Change.*

10. Vernon Jordan, introduction to Robert B. Hill, *The Strengths of Black Families* (New York: Emerson Hall, 1972), ix-x.

11. Nancy Boyd-Franklin, *Black Families in Therapy* (New York: Guilford, 1989), 16. See also Hill, *The Strengths of Black Families;* and Robert B. Hill, *Informal Adoption Among Black Families* (Washington, D.C.: National Urban League, 1977).

12. David A. Anderson, *Kwanzaa* (New York: Gumbs and Thomas, 1993), 56.

13. We developed this definition based on the work of James Garbarino, "Child maltreatment can be defined as acts of omission or commission by a parent or guardian that are judged by a mixture of community values and professional expertise to be inappropriate and damaging." See James Garbarino, "The Incidence and Prevalence of Child Maltreatment," in *Family Violence,* ed. Ohlin and Tonry (Chicago: University of Chicago Press, 1989), 220.

14. James Newton Poling, *The Abuse of Power: A Theological Problem* (Nashville: Abingdon Press, 1991).

15. Here we are thinking of the distinction between anger rape, power rape, and sadistic rape made by Nicholas Groth, *Men Who Rape* (New York: Plenum, 1979), 12-57.

16. "Racism is understood as a system of attitudes, behaviors, and assumptions that objectifies human persons on the basis of color, and that has the power to deny autonomy, access to resources, and self-determination to those persons, while maintaining the values of the dominant society as the norms by which all else will be measured. Although these systems are creations of the social order, they come to be seen as 'natural.' Racism takes personal, institutional and cultural forms and operates at intentional and unintentional, overt and covert levels." The Cornwall Collective, *Your Daughters Shall Prophesy: Feminist Alternatives in Theological Education* (New York: Pilgrim, 1980), 39.

17. See Lee N. June, ed., *The Black Family: Past, Present, and Future: Perspectives of Sixteen Black Christian Leaders* (Grand Rapids, Mich.: Zondervan, 1991), J. Deotis Roberts, *Roots of a Black Future: Family and Church* (Philadelphia: The Westminster Press, 1980).

18. See Talcott Parsons, *Social Structure and Personality* (New York: The Free Press, 1964).

19. See Hester Eisenstein, *Contemporary Feminist Thought* (Boston: G. K. Hall, 1983); Marianne Walters et al., *The Invisible Web: Gender Patterns in Family Relationships* (New York: Guilford, 1988); and Monica McGoldrick et al., *Women in Families: A Framework for Family Therapy* (New York: Norton, 1989).

20. See our discussion of this argument in chapter 2. See also Children's Defense Fund, *The State of America's Children: 1991* (Washington, D.C.: Children's Defense Fund, 1991).

21. "The victims of violence in the home are disproportionately the smaller, the weaker, and the less powerful. Part of their weakness comes from hundreds of years of subordination and being treated as property. Part of the weakness is due to the current social organization of society which offers few places to which victims can flee and live life safely with adequate social resources." Richard Gelles and Murray Straus, *Intimate Violence* (New York: Simon and Schuster, 1988), 32.

22. This section is adapted from White, *Chain, Chain, Change,* 6-8.

23. See David Finkelhor, *Child Sexual Abuse* (New York: The Free Press, 1984), 17-22; and Marie Fortune, *Sexual Violence* (Cleveland: Pilgrim, 1983), 104.

24. For a good discussion of the actual behaviors involved in child sexual abuse, see Diana Russell, *The Secret Trauma* (New York: Basic Books, 1986), 92-101.

25. Incest is "any sexual abuse of a child by a relative or other person in a position of trust and authority over the child.... The important criterion is whether there is a real relationship in the experience of the child." Heidi Vanderbilt, "Incest: A Chilling Report," *Lear's* (February 1992): 221.

26. See Russell, "Brother-Sister Incest: Breaking the Myth of Mutuality," chapter 10 in *The Secret Trauma*, 270-95.

27. "A nonconsenting sexual encounter is one in which an unwilling individual is either pressured or forced into sexual activity by a person in a position of power or dominance. In pressured situations, advantage is taken of a person's vulnerable status, so that refusal to engage in sexual activity may have serious social, economic, or vocational consequences for her. The defining characteristic in forced assault is the risk of injury or bodily harm to the victim should she refuse to participate in sexual activity. Her physical safety is placed in jeopardy." Groth, *Men Who Rape*, 3.

28. For further discussion of the issue of consent, see Marie Fortune, *Sexual Violence* (Cleveland: Pilgrim, 1983); and Marie Fortune and James Poling, *Sexual Abuse by Clergy* (Decatur, Ga.: Journal of Pastoral Care Publications, 1994), 19-20.

29. See Diana Russell, *The Politics of Rape: The Victim's Perspective* (New York: Stein and Day, 1980); also, Diana Russell, *Rape in Marriage* (New York: Macmillan, 1982).

30. *Legal Desk Reference Manual* (Rochester, N.Y.: The District Attorney, n.d.).

31. Audre Lorde, *Sister Outsider* (Trumansburg, N.Y.: Crossing, 1984), 47-48.

32. Wilson, *Crossing the Boundary*, 90.

33. James Garbarino, "The Incidence and Prevalence of Child Maltreatment," in *Family Violence*, ed. Ohlin and Tonry, 220.

34. Cicchetti and Carlson, *Child Maltreatment*, 56.

35. See Ruby F. Lassiter, "Child Rearing in Black Families: Child-Abusing Discipline?" in *Violence in the Black Family*, ed. Hampton, 39.

36. See James Garbarino and Aaron Ebata, "The Significance of Ethnic and Cultural Differences in Child Maltreatment" in *Violence in the Black Family*, ed. Hampton, 21-38.

37. Lassiter, "Child Rearing in Black Families," 44.

38. Ibid., 48-49.

39. Jo-Ellen Asbury, "African-American Women in Violent Relationships: An Exploration of Cultural Differences," in *Violence in the Black Family*, ed. Robert L. Hampton, 90-91.

40. Robert Staples, *Black Masculinity* (San Francisco: Black Scholar Press, 1982).

41. Delores S. Williams, "African-American Women in Three Contexts of Domestic Violence," in *Violence Against Women*, ed. Elisabeth Schüssler Fiorenza and Mary Shawn Copeland (London: SCM Press, 1994), 34.

42. Ibid., 42.

43. Maria Roy, "Four Thousand Partners in Violence: A Trend Analysis," in *The Abusive Partner*, ed. Maria Roy (New York: Van Nostrand, 1982), 17-35.

44. Hampton, *Violence in the Black Family*. See especially chapter 1, "Current Knowledge and Future Research Needs."

45. These figures come from Russell, *The Secret Trauma*, and Finkelhor, *Child Sexual Abuse*.

46. Hampton, *Violence in the Black Family*. See Part II, "Interspousal Violence."
47. Wilson, *Crossing the Boundary.*

4. Stories of Abuse

1. Bell Hooks, *Sisters of the Yam: Black Women and Self-Recovery* (Boston: South End, 1993), 25.
2. Audre Lorde, "A Litany for Survival," in *The Black Unicorn* (New York: W. W. Norton, 1978), 31.
3. Patricia Hill Collins, *Black Feminist Thought: Knowledge, Consciousness, and the Politics of Empowerment* (New York: Routledge, 1990), 235-38, as cited and distilled in James Newton Poling, *Deliver Us From Evil: Resisting Racial and Gender Oppression* (Minneapolis: Fortress, 1996), 106.
4. Poling, *Deliver Us From Evil*, 129.
5. Collins, *Black Feminist Thought*, 21-22.

5. Pastoral Analysis of Abuse

1. There are other published stories of survivors that help to inform our analysis. See Charlotte Vale Allen, *Daddy's Girl* (New York: Wyndham Books, 1980); Maya Angelou, *I Know Why the Caged Bird Sings* (New York: Random House, 1970); Ellen Bass and Laura Davis, eds., *The Courage to Heal: A Guide for Women Survivors* (New York: Harper and Row, 1988); and Ellen Bass and Louise Thornton, *I Never Told Anyone: Writings by Women Survivors of Child Sexual Abuse* (New York: Harper and Row, 1983).
2. Patricia Hill Collins, *Black Feminist Thought: Knowledge, Consciousness, and the Politics of Empowerment* (New York: Routledge, 1990), 92.
3. James N. Poling, *Deliver Us From Evil* (Minneapolis: Fortress, 1996), 103.
4. Ibid., 123.
5. Department of Children and Family Services.
6. The "Imago Dei" as a central concept for the black church has been developed in Wallace Charles Smith, *The Church in the Life of the Black Family* (Valley Forge, Penn.: Judson, 1985), 43-83.
7. "A biosocial perspective suggests that the probability of marital violence increases when ecological instability leads to the erosion of structural buffers.... Common social indicators of marital violence, underemployment, financial pressures, anxiety and alcohol abuse can be conceptualized as markers of ecological instability or its consequences... Even when maltreatment of children is nonadaptive or maladaptive, it occurs more frequently under conditions marked by ecological disturbances associated with rising levels of stress and reliance on coercion in family relationships. Mating and parenting behavior should be especially sensitive to circumstances indicative of ecological instability." Robert Burgess and Patricia Draper, "The Explanation of Family Violence: The Role of Biological, Behavioral, and Cultural Selection," in *Family Violence*, ed. Lloyd Ohlin and Michael Tonry (Chicago: University of Chicago Press, 1989), 59.
8. Robert B. Hill, *The Strengths of Black Families* (New York: Emerson Hall, 1972).
9. Nancy Boyd-Franklin, *Black Families in Therapy* (New York: Guilford, 1989). See also Hill, *The Strengths of Black Families*; and Robert B. Hill, *Informal Adoption Among Black Families* (Washington, D.C.: National Urban League, 1977).
10. See James Comer, "Black Violence and Public Policy," in *American Violence and Public Policy*, ed. Lynn Curtis (New Haven: Yale University Press, 1985), 63-86.

11. See Boyd-Franklin, *Black Families in Therapy.*

12. Some excellent recent books have documented again the effects of economic and class oppression on black families and children. See Jonathan Kozol, *Amazing Grace: The Lives of Children and the Conscience of a Nation* (New York: HarperCollins, 1996); Alex Kotlowitz, *There Are No Children Here: The Story of Two Boys Growing Up in the Other America* (New York: Doubleday, 1991); and William Julius Wilson, *When Work Disappears: The World of the New Urban Poor* (New York: Random House, 1996).

13. Pat Agana, "Training for Life," in *Passion: Discourses on Black Women's Creativity,* ed. M. Sulter (Hebden Bridge, West Yorkshire: Urban Fox, 1990).

14. Angela Davis, *Women, Race, and Class* (New York: Random House, 1983).

15. Michele Wallace, *Black Macho and the Myth of the Superwoman* (New York: Warner Books, 1980), 107.

16. Bell Hooks, *Yearning, Race, Gender, and Cultural Politics* (Boston: South End, 1990), 214.

17. See Diana Russell, *The Secret Trauma: Incest in the Lives of Girls and Women* (New York: Basic Books, 1986).

18. Diana Russell, et al., "The Long-Term Effects of Incestuous Abuse: A Comparison of Afro-American and White Women Victims," in *The Lasting Effects of Child Sexual Abuse,* ed. Gail Wyatt and G. J. Powell (London: Sage, 1988).

19. Carrie Doehring, *Internal Desecration: Traumatization and Representations of God* (Lanham, Md.: University Press of America, 1993).

6. Pastoral Interventions with Victims and Survivors of Abuse

1. We base this insight on the status and role of black pastoral leaders in the black community as well as empirical research that shows that both the black and white population are more likely to talk to a pastor than any other professional. See A. A. Hohmann and D. B. Larson, "Psychiatric Factors Predicting Use of Clergy," in *Psychotherapy and Religious Values,* ed. E. L. Worthington Jr. (Grand Rapids, Mich.: Baker Book House, 1993), 71-84. See also A. J. Weaver, "Has There Been a Failure to Prepare and Support Parish-Based Clergy in Their Role as Front-Line Community Mental Health Workers? A Review," *Journal of Pastoral Care* 49 (1995): 129-49.

2. For further study on issues of family violence in African American families, see Robert H. Hampton, ed., *Violence in the Black Family: Correlates and Consequences* (Lexington, Mass.: Lexington Books, 1987); Evelyn C. White, ed., *The Black Women's Health Book: Speaking for Ourselves* (Seattle: Seal, 1994); Pearl Cleague, *Mad at Miles: A Blackwoman's Guide to Truth* (Southfield, Mich.: The Cleague Group, 1989); and Evelyn C. White, *Chain, Chain, Change: For Black Women Dealing with Physical and Emotional Abuse* (Seattle: Seal, 1985).

3. In emphasizing safety first we are following the wisdom of many counselors in domestic violence, including Judith Herman, *Trauma and Recovery* (New York: Basic Books, 1992), see esp. 155-74.

4. Marie Fortune has most carefully developed the concept of biblical hospitality in relation to domestic and sexual violence. See *Violence in the Family* (Cleveland: Pilgrim, 1986).

5. A good discussion of the need to use "emergency response agencies" in the black community is found in Evelyn C. White, *Chain, Chain, Change,* 36-45.

6. See White, *Chain, Chain, Change,* especially chapter 6, "The Legal System: Blacks and the Legal System," 46-53.

7. See Fortune, *Violence in the Family.*

8. See White, *The Black Woman's Health Book.*

9. Surgeon General Antonia C. Novello, address to an American Medical Association press conference on violence, New York City, 16 January 1992.

10. Herman, *Trauma and Recovery,* 33-50.

11. Ibid., 166-68.

12. Ibid.

13. See David Switzer, *Pastoral Care Emergencies: Ministering to People in Crisis* (New York: Paulist, 1989).

14. The ideas in this section are informed by the discussion of healing in Herman, *Trauma and Recovery,* 175ff.

15. Ellen Bass and Laura Davis, *The Courage to Heal: A Guide for Women Survivors of Child Sexual Abuse* (New York: Harper and Row, 1988).

16. For a good discussion of reconnection in African American families see Nancy Boyd-Franklin, *Black Families in Therapy: A Multisystems Approach* (New York: Guilford, 1989).

17. For good discussions of helping individuals and families recover trust see the work of Edward Wimberly, *African American Pastoral Care* (Nashville: Abingdon Press, 1991). See also by Wimberly, *Pastoral Care in the Black Church* (Chicago, University of Chicago Press, 1978); *Pastoral Counseling and Spiritual Values: A Black Point of View* (Nashville: Abingdon, 1982); and *Using Scripture in Pastoral Counseling* (Nashville: Abingdon Press, 1994).

18. See Herman, *Trauma and Recovery,* especially chapter 11, "Commonality," 214-36. She includes sections on groups for safety, groups for remembrance and mourning, and groups for reconnection.

19. For further discussion of the typical mistakes pastors make with victims and survivors of abuse, see Marie Fortune and James Poling, "Calling to Accountability: The Church's Response to Abusers," in *Violence Against Women and Children: A Christian Theological Sourcebook,* ed. Carol Adams and Marie Fortune (New York: Continuum, 1995), especially p. 452.

20. Annie Imbens and Ineke Jonker, *Christianity and Incest* (Minneapolis: Fortress, 1992).

21. See Marie Fortune, "Forgiveness: The Last Step," in *Violence Against Women and Children,* ed. Adams and Fortune, 201-206.

7. Pastoral Interventions with Perpetrators of Abuse

1. For additional resources on perspectives on perpetrators of violence see: James Poling and Christie Neuger, eds., *The Care of Men* (Nashville: Abingdon Press, 1997), especially chapter 7, "Male Violence Against Women and Children." See also, Jeffrey L. Edleson and Richard M. Tolman, *Intervention for Men Who Batter: An Ecological Approach* (Newbury Park, Calif.: Sage, 1992); Michael Paymar, *Violent No More: Helping Men End Domestic Violence* (Alameda, Calif: Hunter House, 1993); and Morton Patterson, *Broken by You: Men's Role in Stopping Woman Abuse* (Etobicoke, Ontario, Canada: United Church Publishing House, 1995).

2. For a more complete discussion of the denial of perpetrators of violence, see Paymar, *Violent No More,* 86-109.

3. For a discussion of accountability, see Poling, *Deliver Us From Evil* (Minneapolis: Fortress, 1996), 127-32.

4. Paul Laurence Dunbar, "We Wear the Mask," in *American Negro Poetry*, ed. Arna Bontemps (New York: Hill and Wang, 1963), 14.

5. The "Power and Control Wheel" underlying this analysis was developed by the Domestic Abuse Intervention Project, 206 West Fourth Street, Duluth, Minnesota 55806. See Paymar, *Violent No More*, for discussion.

6. For discussion of the legal system, see Evelyn C. White, *Chain, Chain, Change: For Black Women Dealing with Physical and Emotional Abuse* (Seattle: Seal, 1985), especially chapter 6, "The Legal System: Blacks and the Legal System," 46-53.

7. For suggestions on use of emergency services, see White, *Chain, Chain, Change*, 36-45.

8. To find a current list of shelters and emergency services in your area, call: National Hotline on Domestic Violence, 1-800-799-SAFE; Child Abuse/Neglect Hotline, Abuso de Ninos/Mal Cuidado 1-800-252-2873; Elder Abuse/Neglect Hotline, Abuso de Majores/Mal Cuidado, 1-800-252-8966. There are usually hotlines at the state level and in most cities which can be found in the phone book. A readily accessible resource list available to pastoral staff as well as provided for all members of the church is a must.

9. See Paymar, *Violent No More*, for a description of treatment programs for batterers.

10. See Nancy Boyd-Franklin, *Black Families in Therapy* (New York: Guilford, 1989).

11. See Carol Adams, *Woman-Battering* (Minneapolis: Fortress, 1994), 56-58. See also Gus Kaufman, "The Mysterious Disappearance of Battered Women in Family Therapists' Offices: Male Privilege Colluding with Male Violence," *Journal of Marital and Family Therapy* 18:3 (July 1992): 233-44.

12. Carol Adams and Marie Fortune, eds., *Violence Against Women and Children* (New York: Continuum, 1995), 460.

13. This viewpoint is explored by Larry W. Bennett, "Substance Abuse and Domestic Assault of Women," *Social Work* 40:6 (November 1995): 760-69.

8. Congregational Responses for Safety and Healing

1. Linda H. Hollies, "A Daughter Survives Incest: A Retrospective Analysis," in *The Black Women's Health Book: Speaking for Ourselves*, ed. Evelyn C. White (Seattle: Seal, 1990), 82.

2. For a more complete discussion of the issues in this chapter, see Carol Adams and Marie Fortune, *Violence Against Women and Children: A Christian Theological Sourcebook* (New York: Continuum, 1995), especially Part VI: "The Contemporary Church—Pastoral Ministry, Liturgical Issues, and Theological Education," 412-514. See also, Mary Shawn Copeland and Elisabeth Schüssler Fiorenza, eds., *Violence Against Women* (London: SCM Press, 1994); Joanne Brown and Carole Bohn, eds., *Christianity, Patriarchy and Abuse* (Cleveland: Pilgrim, 1989); Mary John Mananzan et al., eds., *Women Resisting Violence: Spirituality for Life* (Maryknoll, N.Y.: Orbis, 1996); and Jeanne Stevenson Moessner, ed., *Through the Eyes of Women: Insights for Pastoral Care* (Minneapolis: Fortress, 1996).

3. Edward P. Wimberly, *Pastoral Care in the Black Church* (Nashville: Abingdon Press, 1979), 22-23.

4. Ibid., 19.

5. Center for the Prevention of Sexual and Domestic Violence, 936 N. 34th Street, Suite 200, Seattle, Washington 98103. Phone: 206-634-1903.

6. Contact your denominational office for a list of materials, or write to Pilgrim Press, 700 Prospect Avenue East, Cleveland, Ohio 44115. Phone: 800-440-3227.

7. Robert M. Franklin, as quoted by Aubra Love, "Way After 'While: Reflections on the Black Church and Domestic Violence Project," *Working Together*. 17:4 (Summer 1997): 2.

8. See Evelyn C. White, *Chain, Chain, Change: For Black Women Dealing with Physical and Emotional Abuse* (Seattle: Seal Press, 1985), especially the section on getting support from the black church, 63-66.

9. For excellent resources see Carol J. Adams and Marie Fortune, eds., *Violence Against Women and Children: A Christian Theological Sourcebook* (New York: Continuum, 1995).

10. White, *Chain, Chain, Change*, 64.

11. Linda Hollies, "A Daughter Survives Incest," 86.

12. Ibid.

13. See Frederick Keene, "Structures of Forgiveness in the New Testament," 121-34, and Marie Fortune, "Forgiveness: The Last Step," 201-206 in *Violence Against Women and Children*, ed. Adams and Fortune.

14. White, *Chain, Chain, Change*, 64-65.

15. See Charles Ess, "Reading Adam and Eve: Re-visions of the Myth of Women's Subordination to Man," 92-120, and Catherine Clark Kroeger, "Let's Look Again at the Biblical Concept of Submission," 141-50, in *Violence Against Women and Children*, ed. Adams and Fortune.

16. For an excellent scholarly commentary on this see Clarice J. Martin, "The *Haustafeln* (Household Codes) in African American Biblical Interpretation: 'Free Slaves' and 'Subordinate Women,'" in *Stony the Road We Trod: African American Biblical Interpretation*, ed. Cain Hope Felder (Minneapolis: Fortress, 1991), 206-31.

17. See Rita Nakashima Brock, "Ending Innocence and Nurturing Willfulness," in *Violence Against Women and Children*, ed. Adams and Fortune, 71-84.

18. Ibid., 108.

19. See Jacquelyn Grant, "The Sin of Servanthood," in *Troubling in My Soul: Womanist Perspectives on Evil and Suffering*, ed. Emilie M. Townes (Maryknoll, N.Y.: Orbis, 1993), 200-205. See also Jacquelyn Grant, "Come to My Help Lord, for I'm in Trouble: Womanist Jesus and the Mutual Struggle for Liberation," in *Reconstructing the Christ Symbol: Essays in Feminist Christology*, ed. Maryanne Stevens (New York: Paulist, 1993).

20. See Delores S. Williams, *Sisters in the Wilderness: The Challenge of Womanist God-Talk* (Maryknoll, N.Y.: Orbis, 1993).

21. Janie Victoria Ward and Jill McClean Taylor, "Sexuality Education for Immigrant and Minority Students: Developing a Culturally Appropriate Curriculum," in *Sexuality in the Curriculum*, ed. James Sears (New York: Teachers College Press, 1992), 183-202.

22. Garth Kasimu Baker-Fletcher, *Xodus: An African American Male Journey* (Minneapolis: Fortress, 1996), 141.

23. Ibid., 141-42.

24. Descriptions of ministry programs in the following section are from "The 1980 Annual Report of Trinity United Church of Christ, Chicago, Ill."

25. R. E. Billingham, "Courtship Violence," *Family Relations* 36 (1987): 283-89. David S. Riggs and Marie Caulfield, "Expected Consequences of Male Violence Against Their Dating Partners," *Journal of Interpersonal Violence* 12:2 (April 1997): 229-40.

26. Diana Russell, *The Secret Trauma* (New York: Basic Books, 1986).

27. See Patricia Davis, *Counseling Adolescent Girls* (Minneapolis: Fortress, 1996).

28. Edward P. Wimberly, "The Men's Movement and Pastoral Care of African American Men," in *The Care of Men*, ed. Christie Cozad Neuger and James Newton Poling (Nashville: Abingdon Press, 1996), 113.

29. Ibid., 114-15.

30. Stephen C. Rasor, "Creating Elder Ministries for Different Locations," in *Honoring African American Elders: A Ministry in the Soul Community*, ed. Anne Streaty Wimberly (San Francisco: Jossey-Bass, 1997), 116.

31. Tanya Fusco Johnson, ed., *Elder Mistreatment: Ethical Issues, Dilemmas and Decisions* (New York: Haworth, 1995). See also the *Journal of Elder Abuse and Neglect*.

32. See James Poling and Marie Fortune, *Sexual Abuse by Clergy* (Decatur, Ga.: Journal of Pastoral Care Publications, 1994); and Marie Fortune, *Is Nothing Sacred?* (San Francisco: Harper and Row, 1989).

9. Concluding Ethical Reflections

1. Lyrics for the traditional African American spiritual "Balm in Gilead," as they appear in *Songs of Zion* (Nashville: Abingdon, 1981), no. 123.

2. J. Deotis Roberts, *Roots of a Black Future: Family and Church* (Philadelphia: Westminster, 1980), 108.

3. Toinette M. Eugene, "Sometimes I Feel Like a Motherless Child: The Call and Response for a Liberational Ethic of Care by Black Feminists," in *Who Cares? Theory, Research, and Educational Implications of the Ethic of Care*, ed. Mary M. Brabeck (New York: Praeger, 1989), 45-61.

4. Alison Jaggar, quoted by Mary Jeanne Larrabee, "Gender and Moral Development: A Challenge for Feminist Theory," in *An Ethic of Care: Feminist and Interdisciplinary Perspectives*, ed. Mary Jeanne Larrabee (New York: Routledge, 1993), 4.

5. See Toinette M. Eugene, "While Love Is Unfashionable: Ethical Implications of Black Spirituality and Sexuality," in *Women's Consciousness, Women's Conscience: A Reader in Feminist Ethics*, ed. Barbara Hilkert Andolsen et al. (Minneapolis: Winston, 1985), 124ff. See also by Eugene, *Black Love Is Black Wealth: The Sacrament of Ordination and a Black, Priestly People*, in the series Crossing Over: Teaching and Celebrating the Sacraments in the Black Churches, ed. Nathan Jones (Chicago: Ethnic Communications Outlet, 1983).

6. See Carol B. Stack, "The Culture of Gender: Women and Men of Color," in *An Ethic of Care*, ed. Larrabee, 110.

7. Eugene, "Sometimes I Feel Like a Motherless Child," 45-46.

8. For a contemporary, selective survey, we strongly recommend the review of all the contributions in "Part VI: The Contemporary Church—Pastoral Ministry, Liturgical Issues, and Theological Education," in *Violence Against Women and Children: A Christian Theological Sourcebook*, ed. Carol J. Adams and Marie M. Fortune (New York: Continuum, 1995), 412-501.

9. Marie Marshall Fortune, *Sexual Violence: The Unmentionable Sin* (Cleveland: Pilgrim, 1983), 42.

10. Stephen L. Carter, *The Culture of Disbelief: How American Law and Politics Trivialize Religious Devotion* (New York: Basic Books, 1993), 29.

11. Ralph Willy, *Why Black People Tend to Shout: Cold Facts and Wry Views from a Black Man's World* (New York: Penguin Books, 1992), 178-79.

12. Roy L. Brooks, *Rethinking the American Race Problem* (Berkeley: University of California Press, 1990), 119-20.

13. See Enoch H. Oglesby, "Folk Proverbs and Faith Formation," in *Born in the Fire: Case Studies in Christian Ethics and Globalization* (New York: Pilgrim, 1990), 18-23.

14. Carter, *The Culture of Disbelief*, 35-36.

15. Ibid., 36-37.

16. See Marian Wright Edelman, *Families in Peril: An Agenda for Social Change* (Cambridge, Mass.: Harvard University Press, 1987).

17. Toinette M. Eugene, "While Love Is Unfashionable," 124-25.

18. For the formulation of these insights, we are indebted to the work of Edward B. Branch's unpublished response to a paper presented by J. Deotis Roberts at a conference on "The Church, Theology, and Violence," sponsored by the Greymoor Ecumenical and Interreligious Institute, New York, 22 October 1994.

19. "Balm in Gilead," in *Songs of Zion*, no. 123.

BIBLIOGRAPHY

I. Books

Adams, Carol, and Marie Fortune, eds. *Violence Against Women and Children: A Christian Theological Sourcebook.* New York: Continuum, 1995.

Adams, Carol. *Woman-Battering.* Minneapolis: Fortress, 1994.

Allen, Charlotte Vale. *Daddy's Girl.* New York: Berkley Publishing Group, 1984.

Anderson, David A. *Kwanzaa.* New York: Grumbs and Thomas, 1993.

Angelou, Maya. *I Know Why the Caged Bird Sings.* New York: Random, 1970.

————. *Gather Together in My Name.* New York: Random, 1974.

————. *Singin' and Swingin' and Gettin' Merry Like Christmas.* New York: Random, 1976.

————. *Heart of a Woman.* New York: Random, 1981.

Archer, John, ed. *Male Violence.* London: Routledge, 1994.

Bambara, Toni Cade. *The Black Woman.* New York: Random, 1980.

Bass, Barbara A., Gail E. Wyatt, and Gloria J. Powell, eds. *The Afro-American Family: Assessment, Treatment, and Research Issues.* New York: Grune and Stratton, 1982.

Bass, Ellen, and Laura Davis, eds. *The Courage to Heal: A Guide for Women Survivors of Child Sexual Abuse.* New York: Harper and Row, 1988.

Bass, Ellen, and Louise Thornton, *I Never Told Anyone: Writing by Women Survivors of Sexual Abuse.* Reprint ed. New York: Harper-Collins, 1991.

Bellah, Robert. *The Broken Covenant: American Civil Religion in Time of Trial.* Chicago: University of Chicago Press, 1992.

Bernard, Jessie. *Marriage and Family Among Negroes.* Englewood Cliffs, N.J.: Prentice Hall, 1966.

Billingsley, Andrew, and Amy Tate Billingsley. *Black Families in White America.* Englewood Cliffs, N.J.: Prentice-Hall, 1968.

Billingsley, Andrew. *Black Families in White America.* Englewood Cliffs, N.J.: Prentice Hall, 1966.

————. *Black Families and the Struggle of Survival.* New York: Friendship Press, 1974.

————. *Climbing Jacob's Ladder: The Enduring Legacy of African-American Families.* New York: Simon & Schuster, 1994.

Billingsley, Andrew, and Jeanne M. Giovannoni. *Children of the Storm: Black Children and American Child Welfare.* New York: Harcourt, Brace, Jovanovich, 1972.

Billson, Janet Mancini. *Pathways to Manhood: Young Black Males Struggle for Identity.* 2d ed. New Brunswick: N.J.: Transaction Publishers, 1996.

Blackwell, James E. *The Black Community: Diversity and Unity.* New York: Dodd, Mead and Co., 1975.

Blassingame, John. *The Slave Community.* New York: Oxford University Press, 1972.

Blount, Marcellus, and George P. Cunningham, eds. *Representing Black Men.* New York: Routledge, 1995.

Bolden, Tonya, ed. *Rites of Passage: Stories About Growing Up by Black Writers from Around the World.* New York: Hyperion Books for Children, 1994.

Bontemps, Arna, ed. *American Negro Poetry.* New York: Hill and Wang, 1963.

Bowman, Thea, ed. *Families: Black and Catholic, Catholic and Black, Readings, Resources, and Family Activities.* Washington, D.C.: U.S. Catholic Conference, 1985.

Boyd-Franklin, Nancy. *Black Families in Therapy: A Multisystems Approach.* New York: Guilford Press, 1989.

Brooks, Roy L. *Rethinking the American Race Problem.* Berkeley: University of California Press, 1992.

Brown, Joanne, and Carole Bohn, eds. *Christianity, Patriarchy and Abuse.* Cleveland: Pilgrim, 1989.

Canon, Katie. *Black Womanist Ethics.* Atlanta, Ga.: Scholars Press, 1988.

Caraway, Nancie. *Segregated Sisterhood: Racism and the Politics of American Feminism.* Knoxville: University of Tennessee Press, 1991.

Carby, Hazel. *Reconstructing Womanhood: The Emergence of the Afro-American Woman Novelist.* New York: Oxford University Press, 1989.

Carter, Stephen L. *The Culture of Disbelief: How American Law and Politics Trivialize Religious Devotion.* New York: Basic Books, 1993.

Cheatham, Harold, and James B. Stewart, eds. *Black Families: Interdisciplinary Perspectives.* New Brunswick: Transaction Publishers, 1990.

Cicchetti, Dante, and Vicki Carlson, eds. *Child Maltreatment: Theory and Research on the Causes and Consequences of Child Abuse and Neglect.* New York: Cambridge University Press, 1989.

Cleague, Pearl. *Mad at Miles: A Blackwoman's Guide to Truth*. Southfield, Mich.: The Cleague Group, 1989.

Cleaver, Eldridge. *Soul on Ice*. New York: Dell, 1970.

Cliff, Michelle. *Claiming an Identity They Taught Me to Despise*. Watertown, Mass.: Persephone, 1981.

Cochran, J., J. T. Stewart, and Mayume Tsutakawa, eds. *Gathering Ground: New Writing and Art by Northwest Women of Color*. Seattle: Seal, 1984.

Collins, Patricia Hill. *Black Feminist Thought: Knowledge, Consciousness and the Politics of Empowerment*. New York: Routledge, 1990.

Comer, James P., and Alvin Poussaint. *Black Child Care*. New York: Simon and Simon, 1975.

Coner-Edwards, Alice F. and Jeanne Spurlock, eds. *Black Families in Crisis: The Middle Class*. New York: Brunner-Mazel, 1988.

Cornwall Collective. *Your Daughters Shall Prophesy: Feminist Alternatives in Theological Education*. New York: Pilgrim, 1980.

Couture, Pamela, and Rodney Hunter, eds. *Pastoral Care and Social Conflict*. Nashville: Abingdon Press, 1995.

Cruikshank, Margaret, ed. *New Lesbian Writing*. San Francisco: Grey Fox, 1984.

Curtis, Lynn, ed. *American Violence and Public Policy*. New Haven.: Yale University Press, 1985.

Davis, Angela. *Women, Culture, and Politics*. New York: Random. 1990.

————. *Women, Race, and Class*. New York: Random, 1983.

Davis, Patricia. *Counseling Adolescent Girls*. Creative Pastoral Care and Counseling Series. Minneapolis: Fortress, 1996.

Davis, Richard A. *The Black Family in a Changing Black Community*. New York: Garland Publishing, 1993.

Dickerson, Bette J., ed. *African American Single Mothers: Understanding Their Lives and Families*. Sage Series on Race and Ethnic Relations, vol. 1. Thousand Oaks: Sage, 1995.

Dobash, R. Emerson, and Russell P. Dobash. *Women, Violence and Social Change*. London: Routledge, 1992.

Doehring, Carrie. *Internal Desecration: Traumatization and Representations of God*. Lanham, Md.: University Press of America, 1993.

Douglas, Kelly Brown. *The Black Christ*. Maryknoll, N.Y.: Orbis, 1994.

DuBois, W. E. B. *The Negro-American Family*. 1908. Reprint, Westport, Conn.: Greenwood, 1970.

————. *The Philadelphia Negro*. 1899. Reprint, New York: Schocken Books, 1967.

————. *The Souls of Black Folk*. 1961. Reprint, New York: Viking Penguin, 1996.

Dyson, Michael Eric. *Between God and Gansta' Rap: Bearing Witness to Black Culture.* New York: Oxford University Press, 1996.

Edelman, Marian Wright. *Families in Peril: An Agenda for Social Change.* 2d ed. Cambridge: Harvard University Press, 1989.

———. *Guide My Feet: Prayers and Meditations on Loving and Working for Children.* New York: HarperCollins, 1996.

———. *The Measure of Our Success: A Letter to My Children and Yours.* New York: HarperCollins, 1993.

Edleson, Jeffrey L., and Richard M. Tolman. *Intervention for Men Who Batter: An Ecological Approach.* Interpersonal Violence Practice Series, vol. 3. Newbury Park, Calif.: Sage, 1992.

Eisenstein, Hester. *Contemporary Feminist Thought.* Boston: G. K. Hall, 1984.

Eugene, Toinette M. "The Black Family That Is Church." In *Family: Black and Catholic,* edited by Thea Bowman, FSPA, 54-60. Washington, D.C.: U.S. Catholic Conference, 1985.

———. "Sometimes I Feel Like a Motherless Child: The Call and Response for a Liberational Ethic of Care by Black Feminists." In *Who Cares? Theory, Research, and Educational Implications of the Ethic of Care,* edited by Mary M. Brabeck, 45-61. New York: Praeger, 1989.

———. "Training Religious Leaders for a New Black Generation." In *Family: Black and Catholic,* edited by Thea Bowman, 121-22. Washington: U.S. Catholic Conference, 1985.

———. "While Love Is Unfashionable: Ethical Implications of Black Spirituality and Sexuality." In *Women's Consciousness, Women's Conscience: A Reader in Feminist Ethics,* edited by Barbara Hilkert Andolsen, et al. Minneapolis: Winston, 1985.

Finkelhor, David. *Child Sexual Abuse.* New York: The Free Press, 1984.

Fishburn, Janet. *Confronting the Idolatry of Family: A New Vision for the Household of God.* Nashville: Abingdon Press, 1991.

Fortune, Marie. *Is Nothing Sacred?* Reprint ed. San Francisco: Harper & Row, 1992.

———. *Sexual Violence: The Unmentionable Sin.* Cleveland: Pilgrim, 1983.

———. *Violence in the Family: A Workshop Curriculum for Clergy and Other Helpers.* Cleveland: Pilgrim, 1991.

Foster, Charles R., and Grant S. Shockley, eds. *Working with Black Youth: Opportunities for Christian Ministry.* Nashville: Abingdon Press, 1989.

Frazier, E. Franklin. *The Negro Family in the United States.* Chicago: University of Chicago Press, 1939.

———. *The Free Negro Family.* 1932. Reprint, Stratford, N.H.: Ayer, 1979.

———. *The Negro Family in Chicago.* Chicago: University of Chicago Press, 1932.

————. *Black Bourgeoisie*. New York: The Free Press, 1965.

Ganley, Anne L., and Carole Warshaw. *Improving the Health Care Response to Domestic Violence: A Resource Manual for Health Care Providers*. San Francisco: The Family Violence Prevention Fund, 1995.

Gary, Lawrence, ed. *Black Men*. Beverly Hills: Sage, 1981.

Gelles, Richard, and Murray Straus. *Intimate Violence*. New York: Simon and Schuster, 1988.

Gibson, William. *Family Life and Morality: Studies in Black and White*. Washington, D.C.: University Press of America, 1980.

Gondolf, Edward W., and Ellen R. Fisher. *Battered Women as Survivors: An Alternative to Treating Learned Helplessness*. Lexington, Mass.: Lexington Books, 1991.

Gondolf, Edward. *Men Who Batter: An Integrated Approach to Stopping Wife Abuse*. Holmes Beach, Fla.: Leaning Publications, 1985.

Grant, Jacquelyn. *White Women's Christ and Black Women's Jesus: Feminist Christology and Womanist Response*. Atlanta: Scholar's Press, 1989.

————. "Come to My Help Lord, for I'm in Trouble: Womanist Jesus and the Mutual Struggle for Liberation," in *Reconstructing the Christ Symbol: Essays in Feminist Christology*, edited by Maryanne Stevens. New York: Paulist, 1993.

Grier, William, and Price M. Cobbs. *Black Rage*. 2d ed. New York: Basic Books, 1992.

Groth, Nicholas, *Men Who Rape*. New York: Plenum, 1979.

Gutman, Herbert G. *The Black Family in Slavery and Freedom, 1750-1925*. New York: Random, 1977.

Hale-Benson, Janice. *Black Children: Their Roots, Culture, and Learning Styles*. Baltimore: Johns Hopkins University Press, 1986.

Haley, Alex. *Roots: The Saga of an American Family*. New York: Doubleday, 1976.

Hampton, Robert, ed. *Violence in the Black Family*. Lexington, Mass.: Lexington Books, 1987.

————. *Black Family Violence: Current Research and Theory*. Lexington, Mass: Lexington Books, 1991.

Hansberry, Lorraine. *To Be Young, Gifted, and Black*. 1970. Reprint, New York: Random, 1996.

————. *A Raisin in the Sun*. 1959. Reprint, New York: Random House, 1994.

Hare, Nathan, and Julia Hare. *The Endangered Black Family*. San Francisco: Black Think Tank, 1984.

Harper, Phillip Brian. *Are We Not Men? Masculine Anxiety and the Problem of African-American Identity*. New York: Oxford University Press, 1996.

Haynes, Norris M. *Critical Issues in Educating African-American Children.* Langley Park, Md.: IAAS Publishers, 1993.

Heggen, Carolyn Holderread, *Sexual Abuse in Christian Homes and Churches.* Scottdale, Pa.: Herald, 1993.

Heiss, Jerold. *The Case of the Black Family: A Sociological Inquiry.* New York: Columbia University Press, 1975.

Herman, Judith. *Trauma and Recovery.* 2d ed. New York: Basic Books, 1993.

Hill, Paul, Jr. *Coming of Age: African American Male Rites-of-Passage.* Chicago: African American Images, 1992.

Hill, Robert Bernard. *Research on African-American Families: A Holistic Perspective.* Boston: William Monroe Trotter Institute, 1989.

———. *The Strengths of Black Families.* New York: Emerson Hall, 1972.

Holland, Joe, and Peter Henriot, S.J. *Social Analysis: Linking Faith and Justice.* 2d ed. Maryknoll, N.Y.: Orbis, 1983.

Hooks, Bell. *Sisters of the Yam: Black Women and Self-Recovery.* Boston: South End Press, 1993.

———. *Yearning, Race, Gender, and Cultural Politics.* Boston: South End Press, 1993.

Hopson, Darlene Powell, and Derek S. Hopson. *Different and Wonderful: Raising Black Children in a Race-Conscious Society.* New York: Prentice Hall, 1990.

Hunter, Rodney J., ed. *The Dictionary of Pastoral Care and Counseling.* Nashville: Abingdon Press, 1991.

Hurston, Zora Neale. *I Love Myself When I Am Laughing. . . and Then When I Am Looking Mean and Impressive: A Zora Neale Hurston Reader,* edited by Alice Walker. Old Westbury, N.Y.: The Feminist Press, 1979.

———. *Tell My Horse.* New York: HarperCollins, 1990.

———. *Their Eyes Were Watching God.* 1978. Reprint, Cutchogue, N.Y.: Buccaneer, 1995.

Imbens, Annie, and Ineke Jonker. *Christianity and Incest.* Minneapolis: Fortress, 1992.

Jarrett-Macauley, Delia, ed. *Reconstructing Womanhood, Reconstructing Feminism: Writings on Black Women.* London: Routledge, 1996.

John Paul II. *Familiaris Consortio: Regarding the Role of the Christian Family in the Modern World.* Washington D.C.: U. S. Catholic Conference, 1982.

Johnson, Dianne. *Telling Tales: The Pedagogy and Promise of African American Literature for Youth.* Contributions in Afro-American and African Studies, no. 139. New York: Greenwood Press, 1990.

Johnson, Ruth W., ed. *African American Voices: African American Health Educators Speak Out.* New York: National League for Nursing, 1995.

Johnson, Tanya Fusco, ed. *Elder Mistretament: Ethical Issues, Dilemmas, and Decisions.* New York: Haworth, 1995.

Jones, Dionne J., ed. *African American Males: A Critical Link in the African American Family.* New Brunswick, N.J.: Transaction Publishers, 1994.

Jones, Jacqueline. *Labor of Love, Labor of Sorrow: Black Women, Work, and the Family from Slavery to the Present.* New York: Random, 1985.

Jones, Nathan, ed. *Crossing Over: Teaching and Celebrating the Sacraments in the Black Churches.* Chicago: Ethnic Communications Outlet, 1983.

————. *God's Good Gift: The Sacrament of Marriage.* Chicago: Ethnic Communications Outlet, 1983.

June, Lee N., ed. *The Black Family: Past, Present, and Future: Perspectives of Sixteen Black Christian Leaders.* Grand Rapids, Mich.: Zondervan, 1991.

King, Victoria, *Manhandled Black Females.* Nashville: Winston-Derek Publishers, 1992.

Kivel, Paul. *Men's Work: How to Stop the Violence That Tears Our Lives Apart.* New York: Ballantine, 1992.

Koss, Mary P., et al. *No Safe Haven: Male Violence Against Women at Home, At Work, and in the Community.* Washington, D.C.: American Psychological Association, 1994.

Kotlowitz, Alex. *There Are No Children Here: The Story of Two Boys Growing Up in the Other America.* New York: Doubeday, 1991.

Kozol, Jonathan. *Amazing Grace: The Lives of Children and the Conscience of a Nation.* New York: HarperCollins, 1996.

Krause, Charlotte, *The Technique of Feminist Psychoanalytic Psychotherapy.* Northvale, N.J.: Jason Aronson, 1993.

Kuklin, Susan. *How My Family Lives in America.* New York: Bradbury, 1992.

Kutenplon, Deborah, and Ellen Olmstead, eds. *Young Adult Fiction by African Americn Writers, 1968-1993: With a Critical and Annotated Guide.* New York: Garland Publishing, 1995.

Ladner, Joyce. *Mixed Families: Adopting Across Racial Boundaries.* Garden City, N.Y.: Doubleday, 1978.

Larrabee, Mary Jeanne, ed. *An Ethic of Care: Feminist and Interdisciplinary Perspectives.* Thinking Gender Series. New York: Routledge, 1992.

Leehan, James. *Pastoral Care for Survivors of Family Abuse.* Louisville: Westminster/John Knox, 1989.

Lenero-Ottero, Luis, ed. *Beyond the Nuclear Family Model: Cultural Perspectives.* Beverly Hills: Sage, 1977.

Levy, Barrie. *Dating Violence.* New Leaf Series. Seattle: Seal, 1991.

Lewis, J., and J. Looney. *The Long Struggle: Well-Functioning Working Class Black Families.* New York: Brunner-Mazel, 1983.

Lincoln, C. Eric, and Lawrence Mamiya. *The Black Church in the African American Experience.* Durham: Duke University Press, 1990.

Lincoln, C. Eric. *The Black Experience in Religion.* Garden City: Anchor Books, 1974.

————. *The Black Church Since Frazier.* New York: Schocken Books, 1974.

Lobel, Kerry, ed. *Naming the Violence: Speaking Out About Lesbian Battering.* New Leaf Series. Seattle: Seal Press, 1986.

Logan, Onie Lee. *Motherwit: An Alabama Midwife's Story.* New York: Dutton, 1989.

Logan, Sadye M. L., Edith M. Freeman, and Ruth G. McRoy, eds. *Social Work Practice with Back Families: A Culturally Specific Perspective.* New York: Longman, 1990.

Lorde, Audre, *The Black Unicorn.* New York: W. W. Norton, 1978.

————. *Sister Outsider: Essays and Speeches.* Trumansburg, New York: The Crossing Press, 1984.

Lystad, Mary, ed. *Violence in the Home.* New York: Brunner-Mazel, 1986.

MacLeod, M., and E. Saraga, eds. *Child Sexual Abuse: Towards a Feminist Professional Practice,* proceedings of conference, April 6-8, 1987, Polytechnic of North London.

Madhubuti, Haki R. *Black Men, Obsolete, Single, Dangerous? Essays in Discovery, Solution, and Hope.* Chicago: Third World Press, 1990.

Mananzan, Mary John, et al., eds. *Violence and Women: The Struggle for Life.* Maryknoll, N.Y.: Orbis, 1996.

Martin, Elmer P., and Joanne Mitchell Martin. *The Black Extended Family.* Chicago: University of Chicago Press, 1978.

Mbiti, John S. *African Religions and Philosophies.* 2d ed. Portsmouth, N.H.: Heinemann, 1990.

————. *The Prayers of African Religion.* New York: Orbis, 1975.

————. *Concepts of God in Africa.* London: SPCK, 1970.

McAdoo, Harriette P. *Black Families.* 3rd ed. Beverly Hills, Calif.: Sage, 1996.

McAdoo, Harriette Pipes, and John Lewis McAdoo. *Black Children.* Focus Editions Series, vol. 72. Newbury Park: Sage, 1985.

McGoldrick, Monica. *Women in Families: A Framework for Family Therapy.* New York: Norton, 1989.

Moessner, Jeanne Stevenson, ed. *Through the Eyes of Women: Insights for Pastoral Care.* Minneapolis: Augsburg Fortress, 1996.

Moraga, Cherrie, and Gloria Anzaldua, ed. *This Bridge Called My Back: Writings by Radical Women of Color.* New York: Kitchen Table, 1981.

Morrison, Toni. *The Bluest Eye.* New York: Washington Square 1972.

————. intro. *Race-ing Justice, Engendering Power: Essays on Anita Hill, Clarence Thomas, and the Construction of Social Reality.* New York: Pantheon Books, 1992.

————. *Sula.* New York: Knopf, 1973.

Morton, Patricia. *Disfigured Images: The Historical Assault on Afro-American Women.* New York: Praeger, 1991.

Moyd, Olin P. *Redemption in Black Theology.* Valley Forge: Pa: Judson 1979.

Moynihan, Daniel Patrick. *Family and Nation.* San Diego: Harcourt, Brace, Jovanovich, 1986.

————. *The Negro Family: The Case for National Action.* Washington, D.C.: U.S. Government Printing Office, 1965.

National Black Child Development Institute. *Who Will Care When Parents Can't? A Study of Black Children in Foster Care.* Washington, D.C.: National Black Child Development Institute, 1989.

Naylor, Gloria. *The Women of Brewster Place.* Contemporary American Fiction Series. New York: Viking, 1983.

Nelsen, Hart M., Raytha L. Yokley, and Anne K. Nelsen. *The Black Church in America.* New York: Basic Books, 1971.

Nelson, James B. *Embodiment: An Approach to Sexuality and Christian Theology.* Minneapolis: Augsburg Fortress, 1979.

Nix, Verolga, and Jefferson Cleveland, eds. *Songs of Zion.* Nashville: Abingdon Press, 1981.

Nobles, W., "Africanity: Its Role in Black Families." *The Black Scholar* 5, 1974.

Nobles, Wade, et al. *African American Families: Issues, Insights, and Directions.* Oakland: Black Family Institute, 1987.

Nobles, Wade, and Lawford L. Goddard. "Black Family Life: A Theoretical and Policy Implication Literature Review." In *The Black Family: An Afrocentric Perspective,* edited by Aminifu R. Harvey New York: United Church of Christ Commission for Racial Justice, 1985.

Obudho, Constance. *Black Marriage and Family Therapy.* Westport: Greenwood Press, 1983.

Oglesby, Enoch H. *Born in the Fire: Case Studies in Christian Ethics and Globalization.* New York: Pilgrim, 1990.

Ohlin, Lloyd, and Michael Tonry, eds. *Family Violence.* Studies in Crime and Justice: A Review of Research Series, vol. 11. Chicago, University of Chicago Press, 1990.

Parsons, Talcott. *Social Structure and Personality.* New York: The Free Press, 1964.

Patterson, Morton. *Broken By You: Men's Role in Stopping Woman Abuse.* Etobicoke, Ontario, Canada: United Church Publishing House, 1995.

Paymar, Michael. *Violent No More: Helping Men End Domestic Abuse.* Alameda, Calif.: Hunter House, 1993.

Perkins, Eugene. *Harvesting New Generations: The Positive Development of Black Youth.* Chicago: Third World Press.

Pinderhughes, Elaine. *Understanding Race, Ethnicity, and Power: The Key to Efficacy in Clinical Practice.* New York: The Free Press, 1989.

Poling, James Newton, *The Abuse of Power: A Theological Problem.* Nashville: Abingdon Press, 1991.

———. *Deliver Us From Evil: Resisting Racial and Gender Oppression.* Minneapolis: Fortress, 1996.

Poling, James Newton, and Christie Neuger, eds. *The Care of Men.* Nashville: Abingdon Press, 1997.

Poling, James Newton and Marie Fortune. *Sexual Abuse by Clergy.* Decatur, Ga.: Journal of Pastoral Care Publications, 1994.

Reid, Kathryn Goering. *Preventing Child Sexual Abuse: A Curriculum for Children Ages Five Through Eight.* Cleveland: Pilgrim, 1994.

Rexroat, Cynthia. *The Declining Economic Status of Black Chldren: Examining the Change.* Washington, D.C.: Joint Center for Political and Economic Studies, 1993.

Roberts, J. Deotis. "The Black Church's Ministry to Families: Priestly Ministry." In *Black Theology Today: Liberation and Contextualization.* New York: Edward Mellon, 1984.

———. *Roots of a Black Future: Family and Church.* Philadelphia: Westminster Press, 1980.

Rodgers-Rose, LaFrances, ed. *The Black Woman.* Beverly Hills: Sage, 1980.

Rose, Susan D. *Keeping Them Out of the Hands of Satan: Evangelical Schooling in America.* New York: Routledge, 1988.

Roy, Maria, ed. *The Abusive Partner.* New York: Van Nostrand, 1982.

Ruether, Rosemary Radford. *New Woman, New Earth: Sexist Ideologies and Human Liberation.* 1975. Reprint, Boston: Beacon, 1995.

Russell, Diana, et al.: "The Long-Term Effects of Incestuous Abuse: A Comparison of Afro-American and White Women Victims," in *The Lasting Effects of Child Sexual Abuse,* edited by Gail Wyatt and G. J. Powell. London: Sage, 1988.

Russell, Diana, *The Politics of Rape: The Victim's Perspective.* New York: Stein and Day, 1980.

———. *Rape in Marriage.* 2d ed. Bloomington: Indiana University Press, 1990.

———. *The Secret Trauma: Incest in the Lives of Girls and Women.* New York: Basic Books, 1986.

Scanzoni, John H. *The Black Family in Modern Society: Patterns of Stability and Security.* Boston: Allyn and Bacon, 1971.

Schecter, Susan. *Women and Male Violence: The Visions and Struggles of the Battered Women's Movement.* Boston: South End Press, 1982.

Sernett, Milton. *Afro-American Religious History: A Documentary Witness.* Durham: N.C.: Duke University Press, 1985.

Shange, Ntozake. *Betsy Brown.* New York: St. Martin's, 1986.

———. *For Colored Girls Who Have Considered Suicide When the Rainbow Is Enuf.* New York: Macmillan, 1989.

———. *Sassafras, Cypress and Indigo.* New York: St. Martin's, 1983.

Shimkin, Demitri, Edith M. Shimkin, and Dennis A. Frate, eds. *The Extended Family in Black Societies.* Hawthorne, N.Y.: Mouton Publishers, 1978.

Slaughter, Diana T., ed. *Black Children and Poverty: A Developmental Perspective.* San Francisco: Jossey-Bass, 1988.

Smith, Barbara. *Home Girls: A Black Feminist Anthology.* New York: Kitchen Table, 1983.

Smith, Karen Patricia, ed. *African-American Voices: Tradition, Transition, Transformation.* Metuchen, N.J.: Scarecrow, 1994.

Smith, Wallace Charles. *The Church in the Life of the Black Family.* Valley Forge, Pa.: Judson, 1985.

Sood, Mary. *African American Parent's Guide: Raising Culturally Aware Children.* Dallas: Amesbury, 1991.

Songs of Zion. Nashville: Abingdon Press, 1981.

Stack, Carol B. *All Our Kin: Strategies for Survival in a Black Community.* 1974. Reprint, New York: Harper Collins, 1983.

Staples, Robert, and Leanor Boulin Johnson. *Black Families at the Crossroads: Challenges and Prospects.* San Francisco: Jossey-Bass, 1993.

Staples, Robert. *The Black Family: Essays and Studies.* 5th ed., Belmont, Calif.: Wadsworth, 1994.

———. *The Black Woman in America: Sex, Marriage, and the Family.* Chicago: Nelson Hall, 1973.

———. *Introduction to Black Sociology.* New York: McGraw-Hill, 1976.

Statman, Jan Berliner. *The Battered Woman's Survival Guide: Breaking the Cycle.* Dallas: Taylor, 1990.

Stevens, Maryanne, ed. *Reconstructing the Christ Symbol: Essays in Feminist Christology.* New York: Paulist, 1994.

Stewart, Ron. *African-American Husbands: A Study of Black Family Life.* Briston, Ind.: Wyndham Hall, 1992.

Stordeur, Richard A., and Richard Stille. *Ending Men's Violence Against Their Partners: One Road to Peace.* Newbury Park, Calif.: Sage, 1989.

Straus, Murray, Richard Gelles, and Suzanne Steinmetz. *Behind Closed Doors: Violence in the American Family.* New York: Anchor Books, 1980.

Sulter, M., ed. *Passion: Discourses on Blackwomen's Creativity.* Hebden Bridge, West Yorkshire: Urban Fox, 1990.

Switzer, David. *The Minister as Crisis Counselor.* 2d ed. Nashville: Abingdon Press, 1986.

Tarpley, Natasha, ed. *Testimony: Young African-Americans on Self-Discovery and Black Identity.* Boston: Beacon, 1995.

Tatum, Beverly Daniel. *Assimilation Blues: Black Families in a White Community.* New York: Greenwood, 1987.

Taylor, Dorothy L. *The Positive Influence of Bonding in Female-Headed African American Families.* New York: Garland, 1993.

Thomas, George B. *Young Black Adults: Liberation and Family Attitudes.* New York: Friendship, 1974.

Thompson, Daniel C. *Sociology of the Black Experience.* Westport: Greenwood, 1974.

Thompson, Mildred I., *Ida B. Wells-Barnett: An Exploratory Study of An American Black Woman, 1893-1930.* Black Women in United States History Series, vol. 15. Brooklyn: Carlson Publishing, 1990.

Townes, Emilie M., ed. *A Troubling in My Soul: Womanist Perspectives on Evil and Suffering.* Maryknoll, New York: Orbis, 1993.

Valora, Washington, and Velma LaPoint. *Black Children and American Institutions: An Ecological Review and Resource Guide.* New York: Garland, 1988.

Walker, Alice, *The Color Purple.* New York: Harcourt Brace Jovanovich, 1982.

———. *In Love and Trouble.* New York: Harcourt Brace Jovanovich, 1974.

———. *In Search of Our Mother's Gardens.* New York: Harcourt Brace, Jovanovich, 1983.

———. *Meridan.* New York: Harcourt Brace Jovanovich, 1976.

———. *The Third Life of Grange Copeland.* New York: Harcourt Brace, Jovanovich, 1970.

———. *You Can't Keep a Good Woman* Down. New York: Harcourt Brace Jovanovich, 1982.

Wallace, Michele. *Black Macho and the Myth of the Superwoman.* New York: Dial Press, 1979.

Walters, Marianne, et al. *The Invisible Web: Gender Patterns in Family Relationships.* New York: Guilford, 1988.

Washington, Mary Helen. *Memory of Kin: Stories About Family by Black Writers.* New York: Anchor Books, 1991.

White, Evelyn C., ed. *The Black Woman's Health Book.* 2d ed. Seattle: Seal, 1993.

———. *Chain, Chain, Change: For Black Women Dealing with Physical and Emotional Abuse.* 2d ed. Seattle: Seal, 1995.

Williams, Delores S. *Sisters in the Wilderness: The Challenge of Womanist God-Talk.* Maryknoll, N.Y.: Orbis, 1993.

Willie, Charles V. *Black and White Families: A Study in Complementarity.* Bayside, N.Y.: General Hall, 1985.

———, ed. *The Family Life of Black People.* Columbus, Ohio: Charles E. Merrill, 1970.

———. *A New Look at Black Families.* 4th ed. Bayside, N.Y.: General Hall, 1991.

Willy, Ralph, *Why Black People Tend to Shout: Cold Facts and Wry Views from a Black Man's World.* New York: Penguin, 1992.

Wilmore, Gayraud S., and James H. Cone, eds., *Black Theology: A Documentary History, 1966–1979.* Maryknoll, N.Y.: Orbis, 1979.

Wilson, Melba. *Crossing the Boundary: Black Women Survive Incest.* Seattle: Seal, 1994.

Wilson, Melvin N., ed. *African American Family Life: Its Structural and Ecological Aspects.* San Francisco: Jossey-Bass, 1995.

Wilson, William Julius. *The Truly Disadvantaged: The Inner City, the Underclass, and Public Policy.* Chicago: University of Chicago Press, 1990.

———. *When Work Disappears: The World of the New Urban Poor.* New York: Random, 1996.

Wimberly, Edward P. *African American Pastoral Care.* Nashville: Abingdon Press, 1991.

———. *Pastoral Care in the Black Church.* Nashville: Abingdon Press, 1979.

———. *Pastoral Counseling and Spiritual Values: A Black Point of View.* Nashville: Abingdon Press, 1982.

———. *Using Scripture in Pastoral Counseling.* Nashville: Abingdon Press, 1994.

Wink, Walter. *Naming the Powers: The Language of Power in the New Testament.* Philadelphia: Fortress, 1984.

Woodard, Charlayne. *Pretty Fire.* New York: Plume, 1995.

Zambrano, Myrna M., *Mejor Sola Que Mal Acompanada: For the Latina in an Abusive Relationship.* New Leaf Series. Seattle: Seal, 1985.

II. Articles

Akbar, Na'im. "Family Stability Among African-American Muslims." In *Muslim Families in North America,* ed. Earle Waugh, Sharon McIrvin

Bibliography

Abu-Laban and Regula Querishi, 213-221. Edmonton: University of Alberta Press, 1991.

Allen, Horace E. "Marriage and Family Counseling with Working Class Blacks." *Urban Mission* 9 (November 1991): 51-58.

Aschenbrenner, Joyce. "Continuities and Variations in Black Family Structure." In *The Extended Family in Black Societies,* ed. Demitri Shimkin and Dennis Frate, 181-200. The Hague: Mouton Publishers, 1978.

Bennett, Larry W. "Substance Abuse and Domestic Assault of Women." *Social Work* 40, (November 1995): 760-69.

Billingham, R. E. "Courtship Violence." *Family Relations* 36, (1987): 283-89.

Blum, Linda M., and Theresa Deussen. "Negotiating Independent Motherhood: Working Class African American Women Talk About Marriage and Motherhood." *Gender and Society* 10, no. 2 (April 1996): 199-212.

Bowles, Dorcas D. "Bi-Racial Identity: Children Born to African American and White Couples." *Clinical Social Work Journal* 21, no. 4 (Winter 1993): 417-28.

Brody, Gene H., Zolinda Stoneman, and Douglas Flor. "Parental Religiosity, Family Processes, and Youth Competence in Rural, Two-Parent African American Families." *Developmental Psychology* 32, no. 4 (July 1996): 696-706.

Brewer, Rose M. "Black Women in Poverty: Some Comments on Female-Headed Families." *Signs* 13, no. 2 (Winter 1988): 331-39.

Brown, Kelly. "A Spirituality of Survival: Helping Our Children Know Who and Whose They Are." *Other Side* 27 (July-August 1991): 20-21.

Chatters, Linda M., Robert Joseph Taylor, and Rukmalie Jayakody. "Fictive Kinship Relations in Black Extended Families." *Journal of Comparative Family Studies* 25, no. 3 (Autumn 1994): 297-312.

Collins, Patricia Hill. "A Comparison of Two Works on Black Family Life." *Signs* 14, no. 4 (Summer 1989): 875-84.

Comer, James P. "Single Parent Black Families." *The Crisis* 90, no. 10 (December, 1983): 42-47.

Dilworth-Anderson, Peggye. "Extended Kin Networks in Black Families." *Generations* 16, no. 3 (Summer 1992): 29-32.

Dyson, Michael. "The Plight of Black Men," *Z Magazine* (February 1989).

Eugene, Toinette M. "African American Family Life: An Agenda for

Ministry Within the Catholic Church." *New Theology Review* 5, no. 2 (May 1992): 33-47.

———. Moral Values and Black Womanists," *Journal of Religious Thought.* (Spring, 1988): 23-34.

Giordano, Peggy C., Stephen A. Cernkovich, and Alfred DeMaris. "The Family and Peer Relations of Black Adolescents." *Journal of Marriage and the Family* 55, no. 2 (May 1993): 277-87.

Guest, Donald Francis. "The Black Church and the Critical Needs of Black Children." *Chicago Theological Seminary Register* 78 (Spring 1988): 16-22.

Hampton, Robert L., and Richard J. Gelles. "Violence Toward Black Women in a Nationally Representative Sample of Black Families." *Journal of Comparative Family Studies* 25, no. 1 (Spring 1994): 105-19.

Hine, Darlene Clark. "Rape and the Inner Lives of Black Women in the Middle West: Preliminary Thoughts on the Culture of Dissemblance." *Signs: Journal of Women in Culture and Society* 14, no. 4 (1989): 912-20.

Hollies, Linda, "A Daughter Survives Incest: A Retrospective Analysis." In *Double Stitch: Black Women Write About Mothers and Daughters,* ed. Patricia Bell-Scott, Beverley Guy-Shefthall, et al., 151-63. Boston: Beacon Press, 1991.

Hunter, Andrea G., and Margaret E. Ensminger. "Diversity and Fluidity in Children's Living Arrangements: Family Transitions in an Urban Afro-American Community." *Journal of Marriage and the Family* 54, no. 2 (May 1992): 418-26.

Hurd, Elizabeth Porter, Carolyn Moore, and Randy Rogers."Quiet Success: Parenting Strengths Among African Americans." *Families in Society: The Journal of Contemporary Human* Services 76, no. 7 (September 1995): 434-43.

Jackson, Jacquelyne J. "Contemporary Relationships Between Black Families and Black Churches in the United States: A Speculative Inquiry." In *Families and Religions,* ed. William D' Antonio and Joan Aldons, 191-220. Beverly Hills: Sage Publications, 1984.

Jayakody, Rukmalie, Linda M. Chatters, and Robert Joseph Taylor. "Family Support to Single and Married African American Mothers: The Provision of Financial, Emotional, and Child Care Assistance." *Journal of Marriage and the Family* 55, no. 2 (May 1993): 261-76.

Jones, LeRoi [Imamu Ameer Baraka]. "A Black Value System." *The Black Scholar* (November 1969).

Kaljee, Linda M., et al. "Urban African American Adolescents and Their

Parents: Perceptions of Violence Within and Against Their Communities. *Human Organization* 54, no. 4 (Winter 1995): 373-82.

Kaufman, Gus. "The Mysterious Disappearance of Battered Women in Family Therapists' Offices: Male Privilege Colluding with Male Violence," *Journal of Marital and Family Therapy* 18, no. 3 (July 1992): 233-44.

Knox, D. H. "Spirituality: A Tool in the Assessment and Treatment of Black Alcoholics and Their Families." *Alcoholism Treatment Quarterly* 2, no. 3-4 (1985): 31-44.

Muse, Daphne. "Black American Classics in Fiction and Poetry for Young Readers." *American Visions* 8, no. 6 (December-January 1993): 33-35.

Peters, Marie F., ed. "Special Issue: Black Families." *Journal of Marriage and the Family* 40, no. 4 (November 1978): 667-828.

Poling, James Newton, "Child Sexual Abuse: A Rich Context for Thinking about God, Community, and Ministry." *Journal of Pastoral Care* 42, no. 1 (Spring 1988): 58-61.

———. "Issues in the Psychotherapy of Child Molesters," *Journal of Pastoral Car* 42, no. 1 (Spring 1989): 25-32.

Riggs, David S., and Marie Caulfield. "Expected Consequences of Male Violence Against Their Dating Partners." *Journal of Interpersonal Violence* 12, no. 2 (April 1997): 229-40.

Stack, Carol B. and Linda M. Burton. "Kinscripts: Reflections on Family, Generation, and Culture." In *Mothering: Ideology, Experience, and Agency,* ed. Evelyn Nakano Glenn, Grace Chang, and Linda Rennie Forcey, 33-44. New York: Routledge, 1994.

Stack, Steven, and Ira Wasserman. "The Effect of Marriage, Family and Religious Ties on African American Suicide Ideology." *Journal of Marriage and Family* 57 (February 1995): 215-22.

Staples, Robert. "Sexual Harassment: Its History, Definition and Prevalence in the Black Community." *The Western Journal of Black Studies* 17, no. 3 (Fall 1993): 143-48.

Stewart, Marsha. "The Influence and Implications of Dr. King's Theology on the Black Church and Its Children." *Journal of the Interdenominational Theological Center* 15, no. 1-2 (1987-1988): 202-10.

Strom, Robert, et al. "Grandparent Education of Black Families." *Journal of Negro Education* 61, no. 4 (Fall 1992): 554-69.

Sudarkasa, Niara. "Female-Headed African American Households: Some

Neglected Dimensions." In *Family Ethnicity: Strength in Diversity,* ed. Harriette McAadoo, 81-89. Newberry Park Sage, 1993.

Taylor, Robert Joseph, Linda M. Chatters, and James S. Jackson. "A Profile of Familial Relations Among Three-Generation Black Families." *Family Relations* 42 no. 3 (July 1993): 332-41.

Twesigye, Emmanuel K. "The Disintegration of the Black Family and the Tragedy of the Nation: The Black Church as God's Primary Answer." In *God, Race, Myth and Power,* ed. Emmanuel K. Twesigye, 109-131. New York: Peter Lang, 1991.

Tyms, James D. "The Black Church as an Ally in the Education of Black Children." *Journal of Religious Thought* 43 (Fall-Winter 1986-1987): 73-87.

Vanderbilt, Heidi. "Incest: A Chilling Report," *Lear's* (February, 1992).

"Violence: The Dark Side of the Family." Special issue of *Journal of Marital and Family Therapy* 18, no. 3 (July 1992): 221-68.

Walls, Carla T. "The Role of Church and Family Support in the Lives of Older African Americans." *Generations* 16, no. 3 (Summer 1992): 33-36.

Williams, Oliver J. "Group Work with African American Men Who Batter: Toward More Ethnically Sensitive Practice." *Journal of Comparative Family Studies* 25, no. 1 (Spring 1994): 91-103.

Wilson, Melvin N., et al. "The Influence of Family Structure Characteristics on the Child-Rearing Behaviors of African American Mothers." *Journal of Black Psychology* 21, no. 4 (November 1995): 450-62.

Zinn, Maxine Baca. "Family, Race, and Poverty in the Eighties." *Signs* 14, no. 4 (Summer 1989): 856-74.

INDEX